Some Moral and Religious Aspects of the War

Some Moral And Religious Aspects Of the War

By

Charles Wood

Minister
Church of the Covenant
Washington, DC

Ross & Perry, Inc.
Washington, D.C.

Reprinted by Ross & Perry, Inc. 2003
© Ross & Perry, Inc. 2003 on new material. All rights reserved.

Protected under the Berne Convention.

Printed in The United States of America

Ross & Perry, Inc. Publishers
216 G St., N.E.
Washington, D.C. 20002
Telephone (202) 675-8300
Facsimile (202) 675-8400
info@RossPerry.com

SAN 253-8555

Library of Congress Control Number: 2001119808
http://www.rossperry.com

ISBN 1-931839-42-5

Book Cover designed by Sapna. sapna@rossperry.com

⊛ The paper used in this publication meets the requirements for permanence
established by the American National Standard for Information Sciences
"Permanence of Paper for Printed Library Materials" (ANSI Z39.48-1984).

EXPLANATORY

THE GREAT WAR has so monopolized thought and speech that to escape from its shadow even in the church has been difficult, if not impossible. With the hope that considering together seriously, neutrally and in a Christian spirit these warring nations and the part they have played and are to play in civilization and progress might possibly prove helpful, the chapters of this unpretentious little book were given as addresses on Sunday evenings, from November to March, in the Church of the Covenant. The only excuse for printing them is that some who heard them were sufficiently interested to arrange for their publication.

CHARLES WOOD

Washington, D. C.
May, 1915

CONTENTS

GERMANY AND THE WAR

"Thou, Oh King, art a King of Kings."   Daniel 2:37.

The German Kaiser rules over more kings than stood at the foot of Nebuchadnezzar's throne. In the confederation of which he is chief, there are four kingdoms —Prussia, Bavaria, Saxony and Wurtemberg. There are six Grand Duchies — each Grand Duke is a near king: one more step up and he sits on his own throne— five Duchies, seven principalities, three free cities—Bremen, Hamburg and Lubeck; and one imperial province, Alsace-Lorraine.

In this great confederation, so very like and yet so very unlike ours, there are 209,000 square miles—about the size of France—which is 60,000 square miles less than our State of Texas, and 588,000 square miles less than Alaska, and 2,954,000 square miles less than the United States, without Alaska. But bigness is not necessarily greatness. The population of these 209,000 square miles is 65,000,000, and the army, on a war footing, is 5,500,000.

Modern Germany is the legitimate successor of the mediæval entity called The Holy Roman Empire. This unnatural union of State and Church governed that section of Europe which we now speak of as Germany for eight hundred and forty-two years. It has been said of it—that it was not an Empire—that it was not Roman—and that it was the very furthest possible removed from being holy.

The modern German Empire is a Prussian product; and Prussia herself, as a dominant power, is of yesterday. It was not until after the victory of Königgratz, in 1866, that the voice of Prussia compelled attention even in Europe; but Prussian history extends its roots very much farther back to a time within a hundred years after William came from Normandy, and, landing on the shores of England, conquered Harold of Hastings, becoming henceforth "William The Conqueror."

In 1170, one hundred and four years after the Norman conquest, a younger son named Conrad left his father's castle of Hohenzollern, in Swabia. "Hohenzollern" means "the high toll or tax place." The castle is in sight from the railway that now passes it. Young Conrad went to the Court of Barbarossa, the great emperor of that day of The Holy Roman Empire, and being very attractive and winning, he advanced rapidly. He married the daughter of the Burggraf of Nuremberg and soon became Burggraf himself. In the constant shuffle, in which kingdoms and principalities were the cards, the successors of this Burggraf found themselves Electors of Brandenburg, known to us as Prussia. From that time the history of Prussia becomes the history of the Hohenzollerns, and the history of the Hohenzollerns is the history of Germany.

The first epoch calling for notice in that history is the Reformation. Martin Luther was a German monk, born in Saxon Eisleben, and dying in Eisleben, but teaching most of his life at Wittenberg, and Wittenberg is on a wide sandy plain 60 miles south of Berlin.

In Martin Luther's day, there was no king in Prussia —only an elector—Joachim II. He fell under the influence of Martin Luther, and many of his people were converts of the new doctrine. This elector did what many other electors and princes of that era did: he took his electorate over with him into the Reformed Church, and from that time Prussia has been nominally Protestant. Whether Joachim himself and the majority of his subjects were really converted, except to Protestantism as a theological system, is very doubtful.

The second epoch is that of the Thirty Years' War, a war more horrible, possibly, even than that which now tears Europe asunder. It was a so-called "Religious War." Men hated each other and killed each other because some were Protestants and some were Romanists —and for no other reason whatever. When that war began, in 1618, there were thirty millions of people living in Germany, and when that war ended, in 1648, there were twelve millions of people left alive. Whole provinces had been desolated and great cities, like Magdeburg, were left without one stone upon another.

The third epoch is that of Frederick the Great. Two Englishmen have written the life of Frederick, in whole or in part, with equal eloquence—Thomas Carlyle and Thomas B. Macaulay. Frederick is Carlyle's hero and Macaulay's detestation. Carlyle said that in a century of chicanery and fraud and lying, Frederick was the one man who dared to be true. Macaulay said "That in order to rob a neighbor—Maria Theresa

7

—whom he had promised to defend, black men fought on the coast of Coromandel and red men scalped each other on the Great Lakes of North America."

Frederick the Great is confessedly the ideal of William the Second, and the character of William the Second is, perhaps, equally problematic.

The fourth epoch is that of the Napoleonic Wars. When we Americans read the story of the wars of Napoleon we are pro-German and pro-Prussian, at least *pro tem.* Beautiful and unhappy Queen Louise, as she comes down the stairway in the picture that hangs in every German gallery, and copies of which are in every German home—walks straight into our hearts. When she weeps, after the overwhelming defeat of Jena, only asking Napoleon that her country might not be utterly crushed, we weep with her and wish that she might have been king in the place of her timid husband. Napoleon, as he stood by the tomb of the great Frederick, said, so the story runs, "Had *he* been alive, we would never have been here." Had Queen Louise worn the crown, Napoleon might never have conquered Prussia.

When she pleaded with Napoleon that the kingdom might not be dismembered, he smiled a sardonic smile, and wrote in his diary that, in spite of her beauty and tears, she got nothing from him. When she crouches hopeless beside the broken carriage, in which she had fled with her two boys, while the enemy is in hot pursuit, we look away with dimmed eyes. Fifty-five years later the younger of those boys stands, not as a captive, but as a conqueror, in Versailles, and there, amid his generals, his princes and his kings he is crowned *Emperor of Germany,* within the walls covered with

8

great paintings depicting the victories of Napoleon and the shame of Prussia!

The fifth epoch is that of modern Germany, which began with that coronation in 1871 in the French Capital.

The twenty-six units of modern Germany are combined together more closely than the units which make up our Republic. They have a President for life, and he is already chosen before he is born. As long as the family of Hohenzollern shall continue to exist, and Germany shall hold to its confederation, the oldest son of the reigning Hohenzollern inherits the imperial crown.

It was my great privilege, in the winter of 1878-9, to be a student in the University of Berlin, and I am frank to say that I became as thorough a German as it is possible for a man to be who has very little aptitude for the German tongue, and who considers German philosophy and German beer equally impossible. The most memorable incident of that winter was the return of the Emperor, William the First—whom the Germans have always tried to call "William the Great," without much success. The homecoming of the Emperor after his restoration to health—the assassin had almost taken his life, and he had been away for some months—was a national festival. He came back to Berlin with Bismarck, by whose diplomacy and by whose duplicity Germany had been made an empire and he had been made an Emperor. With him were all the royal family, and all the great generals who had fought in the Franco-Prussian War, and the reception the people gave their Emperor was little short of adoration.

If only his son, Frederick the Good, had lived—if only he had lived! But those short days of his reign passed before he had time to work out any of the reforms that filled his heart. Then came to the throne of Prussia, and to the imperial throne of Germany, the grandson of the first William, William the Second, a man whose abilities are undoubtedly greater than those of his grandfather, but whose philanthropy is undoubtedly less than his father's.

We cannot understand what the Emperor is to the German people. If only our "Uncle Sam" were not a caricature; if he were more of a real father, if he were the embodiment of all that we mean by our flag and our national hymn—"My Country, 'Tis of Thee"—if he were all this at one and the same time, he would be to us what the German Emperor is to the German people. He is not a person. He is a personification, an ideal.

After William the Second came to the throne he very soon "dropped his pilot," the great Bismarck, who died of a broken heart like Napoleon, and like every man who lives simply for dominion and power. He confessed, in his Reminiscences, that he had instigated three great wars— the war against Denmark, the war against Austria, and the war against France—and had done many other noteworthy and notorious things, but life had been far from satisfying.

After dropping the pilot, William the Second took the helm and gave the signal "Full speed ahead," and the response was instantaneous. Germany, during his reign, has broken all old world records. The Germans, when William came to the throne, were an agricultural people. Soon a great stroke of good fortune came to them in a most unexpected way. I remember hearing the American Consul at Mannheim say to one of his German friends, "You are really eating the bones of your ancestors. There is not a

10

square inch of your land that has not been exhausted, and all the nutriment that comes from it is from ancestral nitrates."

It is not a pleasant thought, but nevertheless it was only too true. A few decades ago, owing to a bad debt—it is said—in Chile, Germany found herself possessed of a strip of desert land along the western coast of Chile, running up into Peru, and these lands were found to be incalculably rich in nitrates. There are no taxes in Chile. The revenue is raised from the nitrate beds. Whenever any one in Chile suggests anything that ought to be done by civic contributions and generosity, everyone else reminds them of the nitrate beds. These Chilian nitrate beds were a tremendous boon for Germany. They doubled her harvest. It was as if she had added an acre to every acre she then possessed. When .we ask why emigration to the United States from Germany is so much less than twenty-five years ago the answer is largely to be found in the nitrate beds of Chile.

Germany's agricultural gains delayed, but did not prevent, her transformation from an agricultural to an industrial community. In her industries and manufactures she has showed more than Yankee. ingenuity. When her manufacturers found that in India all the egg cups coming from England were much too large for the small eggs of India, the Germans made egg cups to fit the eggs—and there is not an English egg cup for sale in all India today.

When the Africans insisted on using English scissors, made at Sheffield, with fine, sharp points, in the place of razors as weapons of defence and offence, the English paid no attention to the slaughter, but the Germans sent out

11

round, dull-pointed scissors, useless as weapons, and no other scissors are now used in Africa.

When the South Americans, from Peru all the way to Chile, and from Chile all the way up to Brazil, wanted certain kinds of goods with pink ribbons, and certain other kinds of goods with iron bands—Englishmen and Americans said "nonsense," but the Germans delivered the goods and drove the Englishmen and Americans from those markets.

It was said in Goethe's time that the gods had given the land to France, the sea to England, and the air to Germany. But we Americans taught Germany how to conquer the air with our aeroplanes, and then, with her extraordinary aptness, she went much beyond her teacher and made better aeroplanes and dirigibles—of which we have none—and with them she has conquered the air, and now she thinks it would be as well, incidentally, to conquer the sea and the land. She has already, partly, conquered the sea. She is second only to England in her commerce, and she surpasses England in the North German Lloyd and the Hamburg-American lines—the two greatest steamship lines in the world.

Germany has done not a little, also, in conquering the land. German roads are as good as French roads—and French roads are supposedly the best in the world. German hotels, of which, years ago, many American and English travelers found much fault, are far better than French hotels—in the smaller cities at least. The German towns are incomparably cared for, and the German trees in all the municipalities are only excelled by the trees in our own city.

The greatest names in Germany are not the names of marshals and admirals—for which we thank God—they are the names of philosophers like Leibnitz and Lotze; of poets like Goethe and Schiller; of historians like Mommsen and Mosheim; of scientists like Von Humboldt and Roentgen. But the greatest name in German history, many think, is the name of the greatest of the world's reformers, Martin Luther, whose hymn is still sung in our churches with delight.

But this modern Germany has been drinking very deep of the cup of which we have been glad to drink all that it was possible for us to secure for our own personal use— the very inebriating cup of prosperity. In that cup there is a deadly poison. It is the poison of materialism, and that poison manifests itself by different symptoms. Here in America the Germans tell us it has manifested itself in Mammonism, the worship of the almighty dollar, and they charge us with caring for nothing but money. They are not conscious that they have the same poison in their veins. It shows itself in Germany by what we call militarism— but it is the same poison.

We have been a little less responsive to that poison than the Germans, because we have breathed better air. Our environment has been more favorable. We have never known what it was to be "cribbed, cabined and confined." When we want to stretch, we stretch out toward Alaska, and our children's children's children may continue to stretch without any danger. But when the German giant wants to stretch, where is he going to stretch to? He says, "These Lilliputians," as he calls them, "have closed all the doors." "They have shut the door to the Adriatic, and, during the last war, to the opulent East via the Bagdad Railway. They have left two or three little apertures on the Baltic, and a slit, the Kiel Canal, for which I paid half as much as you

13

paid for the Panama Canal, which gives me an entrance into the North Sea, and I have one or two small ports besides, but I can scarcely breathe. I am the world's greatest military power—you Americans say so, and it must be so—but, commercially, I am in Egyptian bondage to England."

At that opportune or inopportune moment came Mephistophelian militarism wearing a helmet and sword, and hissing, "There are but two alternatives for you—dominion or death." Later militarism came in the guise of a philosopher, calling himself Nietzsche or Treitschke, or Bernhardi. Philosophic militarism pushed out the old idealistic philosophy that made the German for so many centuries seemingly a dreamer, remote from the practical affairs of men. Each of this modern trio teaches that war is righteous, that war is a necessity for a people that would not grow soft and effeminate.

The poison of this materialism has hardened the arteries of Germany, and if you would see the proof of it, you need not to England or France look for it, but go to Germany and look at her art. Look at her Sieges Säule, her column of Victory, flaunting itself in the Thiergarten, the park of Berlin! Look at that long row of amazing statues of conquerors, or would-be conquerors, in the same park, and compare their floridness with the simplicity of Frederick the Great's statue in Unter den Linden. If you are not satisfied, go to the little city of Worms, and stand beneath the superb statue of Martin Luther, the man of the Book, and surrounded with men like himself, men with the Book —all reformers and teachers and prophets. Then take the rapid express train—there are few more rapid or better in the world—to Hamburg, and stand there under the statue of "the man of blood and iron," Von Bismarck. The great

Chancellor, girdled about seemingly by cannon, with a great
sword at his side and fire flashing from his stern eyes, is
the incarnation of the philosophic militarism of Nietzsche,
Treitschke and Bernhardi which he foresaw and feared.
It is as if we had erected here a colossal statue to George
Washington in the guise of a multi-millionaire.

> " 'Tis but the moral of all human tales,
>   'Tis but the oft-repeated story of the past:
> First freedom, then glory; when that fails,
>   Wealth, vice, corruption, barbarism at the last."

Goethe said: "It is only a little while ago that we Germans were barbarians." That does not matter much. It is
only a little while ago that we Americans, wherever our
ancestors came from, were barbarians. What does matter
is this: How long will it be before Germany or America,
passing swiftly from freedom to glory, shall come to wealth
—we are in that stage or near it now, some think—to vice,
corruption, and at the last—barbarism?

"This war," the young Crown Prince says, "is the most
unnecessary and useless that has been fought in modern
times." It is the most unnecessary and useless and criminal,
probably, that has ever been fought. But if they who pro-
fess to be Christians, in Germany, England, France, Russia
and Austria, would but pray—and supposedly they are all
men of prayer—not "my kingdom come," but "Thy kingdom come," and if that prayer were echoed by their marshals and admirals and by their soldiers in the trenches,
might not the hour come speedily—if the peoples of those
lands, and the peoples of the whole world would join that
prayer, meaning what they say—when a flag of truce would

be sent out, and these armed millions would rise from the trenches and fling down their guns and grasp each other's hands, crying: "Brothers all! Sons of the same Father! We cannot kill each other!" You say it is incredible; that it is fantastic and visionary! We heard here, from this very pulpit, this afternoon of modern miracles in China, where a wall greater than the Great Wall, the impenetrable wall around the *Literati,* the scholar class, suddenly fell in the midst of the Boxer uprising, and multitudes of the class which had spurned Christianity with unspeakable scorn, turned to Christ, giving up the sage Confucius for the lowly Nazarene.

Miracles! "Men of blood and iron," you say, these rulers of Europe are, but blood is thicker than water; and iron, when you strike it with iron, rings and flashes, and when you heat it, it grows red and hisses with its heat, but when you raise the temperature a little more the hard iron melts and mingles with all the melting iron around, and who can tell then whether it was iron from Germany, Russia, England or France? Ah! If these men would only pray! The diplomats say there are great difficulties—impossibilities—in the way of peace! There is only one difficulty—the lack of love. Let them but love. Let them but come together in love, and each might have all they want without shedding a drop of blood. Germany might get those last sixty miles of the Rhine, and her ships could float untroubled to the sea; France might get back Alsace-Lorraine; England might keep what she has—she has enough—and Russia might go down to Constantinople and make it a free city like Hamburg, Lubeck or Bremen —and the Turks might be glad to retire to the quiet safety of Mecca! It only means a little raising of temperature, and it is done.

16

What Germany needs—this wonderful Germany—is not more schools, for her schools are among the best in the world. She has only one per cent of illiteracy. Her universities have drawn the best scholars of England and America, who count it a high privilege to sit in her lecture halls—what Germany needs is not more science or philosophy; not even more music; but what she needs is another reformer like Martin Luther, a man fearless before kings, princes and emperors, a man who shall call the people back, not to the god of Joshua, or Gideon, or Judas Maccabaeus, a god of war—it is dangerous to speak of such a god in Germany—but to the God and Father of Our Lord, Jesus Christ; a man who shall dare to say, in court and camp, as well as in church, that God rules in the heavens and on earth, and that it shall not profit a man, be he Kaiser, King or serf, to win the world and lose the holy fire that burns in every man's soul until it is extinguished. That great as Germany is—and France, and England, and Russia, and Austria, and the United States—if any one of them, or all of them combined, shall dare to break the laws of God, they shall each and all utterly perish.

17

ENGLAND AND THE WAR

"Sing unto the Lord a new song, and His praise from the end of the earth, ye that go down to the sea, and all that is therein; the isles, and the inhabitants thereof." Isaiah 42:10.

For all who read English history, primarily as Americans and secondarily as students, the history of England begins not with the Picts and Scots, nor with Hengist and Horsa, and their half-civilized Saxons conquering the scarcely less civilized savages; nor with King Egbert, who, more than a thousand years ago, named that little island "England"—but it begins in a sleepy little valley in Surrey, not far from Windsor, where, on a summer's day in 1215, the Barons wrung from King John the Magna Charta, and at the same time unconsciously and unintentionally won a victory for liberty and democracy the world over. This victory is of more interest to us as Americans than the far more splendid triumphs gained by the English armies in France, at Crecy and Poitiers and Agincourt.

Through many volumes of English history we pick our way along a narrow path stained with blood, winding in and out among "Wars of the Roses" and innumerable other wars of less lovely names, and close to "The Field of the Cloth of Gold," and underneath the windows of King Henry VIII's gorgeous palaces filled with tragedies of dethroned and beheaded queens, till the light begins to grow brighter on the path leading to still greater triumphs for democracy and liberty and broadens and glows with a lurid glare flung upon it by torches held in the hand of a Pym, a Hampden and a Cromwell. Then England becomes for a time a Republic, and for all time, at the heart of her, a democracy, in spite of a Roman Catholic reactionary James and four Hanoverian Georges with mediæval dreams of unlimited sovereignty.

In Hayden's Dictionary of Dates, "For American Readers," there is no reference whatever, so far as I can find, to the sailing of the "Mayflower." Yet, when that little ship turned her prow westward, on that September day in 1620, from the port of Plymouth, sailing onward, she knew not where, it was assuredly one of the most significant events in English history.

Those 102 men, women and children on board that little ship, in quarters which even our refugees from Europe this summer would have spurned as impossible, made up the most memorable passenger list of any vessel that has ever crossed the Atlantic. That coming of the "Mayflower" was the most significant of all crossings made thus far or that ever will be made, it may be, over that sea, though it is quite within the realm of possibility that this coming summer or the summer after, or as soon as the war shall cease, the airship "America," or the airship "Europe," for so she may be called by that time, will sail from Newfoundland to the Azores, and from the Azores to that same Plymouth in old England from which the Pilgrims began their real journey.

When the Pilgrims landed at Plymouth they brought all their treasures with them, though, all told, everything they had, including the ship in which they came, could not have been sold for enough in that day, or even in ours, to have purchased one big gun necessary for the protection of the rock on which they landed, from a twentieth century Dreadnaught. Yet the treasures they carried with them far surpassed in value all the wealth of "Ormus or of Ind."

"The Pilgrim," as George William Curtis says, "was narrow and bigoted, sour, hard and intolerant, but he was the man for whom God had sifted three kingdoms to find seed grain to plant a new republic, and he has done more for humanity than any other man in history;"—in American history unquestionably.

He brought on the tip of his tongue the English language, though he was not the first to bring it, the language of Chaucer and Shakespeare, the most plastic and facile instrument the world has yet found for trade and commerce and for the expression of the deepest thoughts of the human soul. That language in the last three decades has spread far more rapidly than any other tongue. A French orator, speaking to 10,000 people in the Hippodrome at Paris, said, "In order to be understood by the largest number present, I will use the English language." And in whatever capital you go, of whatever land, you find the English language the most useful medium for the exchange of ideas, though other tongues may be better for concealing thought.

The Pilgrim brought with him, beside the English language, English literature. There were very few copies, doubtless, of the English Bible on board the "Mayflower," but the Pilgrim knew his Bible mostly by heart. On some of our great ocean liners there are Bibles in every stateroom. This is a contrast to the "Mayflower"—but it might be you would find a still greater contrast if you should examine the passengers as to their knowledge of the Bible. There may have been no copy of Shakespeare on board— though he had been dead but four years—but constructively

21

the Pilgrim brought with him Chaucer and Shakespeare. Milton and Wordsworth, Tennyson, Browning and Kipling. All the great English poets have been Puritan at heart, for they have all sung of righteousness, of liberty, of God, and the divine right of the people as opposed to the divine right of kings. Matthew Arnold did not like the Puritans —though his father was a Puritan—and he said many unpleasant things about Puritanism. But, in spite of himself, his Puritan pen, like Balaam's tongue when he started to curse Israel, was compelled to bless, and no man has spoken more sympathetically of all that was essentially Puritan than Arnold.

The Pilgrim brought with him English law, as well as literature, like the Virginia Companies. His Town Meeting was simply a reproduction, in a very rude form, of the English Parliament.

Years ago an American went through Westminster Abbey with Dean Stanley and a company of working men—such a company as Dean Stanley was accustomed to take through the Abbey every month. This group proved to be Non-Conformists from Christ Congregational Church. When they came into the Chapter House the Dean said, "Here, under this roof, constitutional liberty was born." And then, with a smile, turning to the American, he said, "Even our young friend cannot deny that." "Long before the Commons were accustomed to meet at Westminster they met here and fought their battles for their rights, and for ours" —and the American might have added, "and for ours, too."

Our government, so the Unitarian historian, Bancroft, says, was organized on the model of the government of the Presbyterian Church, and the Presbyterian Church, though it goes back, of course, to Calvin and the Huguenots and the Waldensees and the Culdees of Iona, and to the Jewish synagogue, with its elders, received the imprint of Great Britain, not only at the hands of Knox, but far more at the hands of the Westminster Assembly, meeting in the Jerusalem Chamber of the Abbey and issuing from the sacred precincts of Westminster the Confession of Faith and the Catechism.

Those were the days in which the Established Church of England was Presbyterian. From 1646, after the defeat of Charles I at Naseby, to 1655, three years before the death of Cromwell, Presbyterianism was the State Church.

The Pilgrim, like the Puritan, who came after him, was English to the very marrow of his bones. He built his house on English plans and tried to make it as much as possible like the house he had left in England under compulsion. His clothes were English, even though they were made by his wife. They were the exact pattern of the garments worn in England in Cromwell's time. His manners, his customs and his culture were all English. He had the English feeling for his wife and daughter, different from the feelings of husbands and fathers on the Continent. His descendants here, finding they were on the right track, have gone so far as to place woman on a pedestal called the world over—"American"—no rights reserved.

When the Pilgrim left England only Pilgrims wept. He was like an eaglet who was pushed by the eagle out of the nest. Even when the thirteen colonies, from Massachusetts to Georgia, lifted their hands against the mother country, and, in a single year, three millions of what we are accustomed to think were the best Englishmen then alive, and more than 2,000,000 square miles of territory prospectively were torn away from England, she did not stop to mourn over it; she had no time to waste. There were other things to be done. She heard "the call of the wild" from far distant lands. She saw that her "manifest destiny" was pointing to the Orient, and there she found a vast continent peopled not by a few millions, but by hundreds of millions.

England conquered India. If it were not historic it would be incredible. A few thousand Englishmen conquered these hordes ruled by maharajahs, many of whom were richer than European kings. They had vast armies, with innumerable elephants. Pizarro conquered Peru; Cortez conquered Mexico; but the conquest of India by England was far more wonderful—when we think, not of the conquest only, but of the results of the conquest as well.

Pizarro sucked the lifeblood of Peru, and Cortez was a vampire, who fastened on the throat of Mexico. Neither of those lands has yet recovered from the merciless exploitation of her territory and her treasures. But England transfused her blood into the sluggish current of the Hindus; lifted up a great continent to a level if not as high as Europe, yet far higher than any people in Asia have ever attained unaided.

England civilized Australia, another continent, and New Zealand. England cultivated Canada—great Canada—until Canada has reached the point—to our shame be it said—when thousands of our best farmers have forsaken our Northwest for her's.

England has changed Egypt from wretchedness and hopeless poverty, brought about by inhuman injustice and indifference, to one of the richest of earth's provinces.

On the 9th of August, in 1902, I stood on a balcony just opposite the entrance to Westminster Abbey and saw

King Edward VII and his Queen Alexandra, in their Cin-
derella coach of glass and gold, with a great retinue about
them, come to the gates of the Abbey and disappear within
its long-drawn aisles for their coronation. Returning from
the Abbey, and making their way slowly through the streets,
cheers rang on every side for the King and the Queen, and
for Lord Roberts, the military idol of the hour. But the
wildest cheers were for the representatives of the colonies,
three thousand, five thousand, seven thousand, twelve thousand miles away from England, and the loudest cheers of all
greeted the Hindu princes in their gorgeous oriental costumes. They had come all the way from India with their
great retinues at their own expense, not under compulsion,
not dragged, like Thusenelda in a Roman triumph, but voluntarily, as the expression of the loyalty of their hearts, and
of their belief that India, conquered as she was, has found in
her conqueror a benefactor and preserver necessary to her
very existence.

Intense as was the loyalty of that coronation day, it has
been a hundredfold increased, I am told, by King Edward's
son, George V, who, when at Delhi for his Durbar—or second coronation—announced that the European capital at
Calcutta, had been removed to the old Mogul Mohammedan
capital of Delhi. In addition it was proclaimed that the civil
service, the finest in the world, of which our service in
Porto Rico, and the Philippines is a far-off imitation—
that this civil service, to which England for decades has
given her best men, was to be far more widely opened
both to Hindu and Mohammedan.   Further, that the
Victoria Cross, the most coveted honor that can be given
to an English subject, noble or commoner, was to be given
henceforth alike to Hindu or Mohammedan who shall have

earned it by extraordinary personal bravery on the field of battle. Only the other day news came that a Mohammedan soldier in the trenches in Belgium, when all his comrades had been killed, fought single-handed against ten of his foes, who rushed upon him with their bayonets, and though he was rescued alive, there was scarcely an unwounded spot upon his breast large enough to hold the medal he had won.

While England was conquering, colonizing, civilizing and cultivating all over the earth, she was not forgetful of her own garden at home. During the last century she has become easily one of the chief—many say the chief—commercial and intellectual powers of the world. Her Lombard Street "is the center from which all the threads of trade move out like a golden web to the uttermost ends of the earth." Her roll of scientists and scholars has on it such names as Newton, who discovered the law of gravitation, and in a single day changed whole groups of sciences; and Darwin, who detected the method of evolution which runs from the lowest to the highest life—the method of progress if not of creation; and Watts, who discovered the genii imprisoned in steam; and Stevenson, who captured these genii and enslaved them in the engine rooms of steamships, and in the machinery of locomotives, thus multiplying indefinitely the effectiveness of man.

What is this England today? This England, with these vast possessions? This England that numbers among her subjects one-fifth of the human race? Is she a colossal octopus, lifting her monster head with a billion eyes above the sea, looking greedily for islands and for continents about which she may wrap her countless tentacles, and drag them down into her insatiable maw? Or is England an organism wholesome and essential to the vitality and the welfare of the human race?

The difference between an octopus and an organism—not scientifically, of course, but practically—is that an octopus grabs and never gives, and that an organism gets and gives like the systole and the diastole of a healthy heart, getting and giving its blood back to all the extremities. In the last decade England has, it is true, received much, but she has given four millions of her stalwart sons and her stately daughters to her colonies and to the United States. She has distributed her capital in millions, and hundreds of millions, and billions—American billions—not English—to South America, to the United States, to Canada, and where else in all the world who can tell? She has given us here in America—somewhat grudgingly, perhaps —some of her very greatest preachers to stimulate our religious and spiritual life. She gave us John Hall and William M. Taylor, and only the other day John Henry Jowett and G. A. Johnston Ross. What is this England? An octopus or an organism?

This England now finds herself fighting in the greatest war the world has ever seen. Oh! let us pray to God that it may be the greatest war, the last great war, the world will ever see!

Already England has received, as her enemies would say —"according to her wont"—great gains even from this war. It is proving a caustic, burning out abnormal and malignant growths which are quite as pronounced, some of them, in the daughter as in the mother.

First, the war has already burned out the malignant growth of arrogance. The great essayist and historian,

James Anthony Froude, writing about England and her colonies forty-four years ago, mentions this among her most pronounced, most pernicious, and most irritating characteristics. It is a quality that has made the English disliked in many quarters of Europe, and it is a quality that has made the American disliked in every part of South America.

Second, this caustic of war has burned out her secularism—not only an undue love of money, which we Americans think was always more pronounced in England than in America, but an undue love of sport. Kipling saw it, and for a day or two he was the most unpopular man in England when he dared to speak of the "flanneled fools at the wicket and the muddied oafs at the goal," striking at the two national games of England, cricket and football, as baseball and football are our two national amusements, and drawing off here as in England, as Kipling believed, much vitality and energy that might be much more profitably used in more serious ways.

That phase has passed in England. More than 100,000 football players have gone to the war, not as conscripts, but as volunteers. England is as serious today as in the days of Wesley or Whitfield—the centennial of whose marvelous ministry is being commemorated today in very many of the churches of America.

Third, the caustic of war has burned out her sectionalism. She was becoming sectionalized. One segment of society was lifting its hand against another segment. In England the women were fighting against the men, and in Ireland Protestants were fighting Roman Catholics, and Roman Catholics were fighting Protestants, and both were ready to lift their hands against England when England should prove not to be on their side.

28

India, too, a year or so ago was on the eve of a mutiny, it was feared. Mutiny means much more to English ears than to ours. The word still makes the English heart tremble. It recalls the horrors of 1857. A mutiny today in India would be a thousandfold more awful than in that earlier day, when there were fewer English women and children there.

The caustic of war has burned out all these sorts of sectionalism. What has become of the militants of England and the militants of Ireland, and the mutiny of India? Indian princes, both Mohammedan and Hindu, have not only given their subjects, but themselves, together with their long-hoarded treasures, to England. They are mingling their blood with English blood in a brotherhood not to be broken. If nothing else comes to England from this war than what has come already, she has been in a large part repaid for the stupendous sacrifices she has been compelled to make.

But, better still, England has been brought to her knees by the war. Not by defeat, nor by the fear of it, but by her conscious need of God.

From the English King on his throne to the English cobbler at his bench and the soldier in the trenches, one prayer has gone up from the true Protestant, Puritan, Christian heart of England that Christ's Kingdom may come, whatever may be England's lot, small or great, in the extension of it. When sovereign and subject pray such a prayer, it cannot be unanswered, when with the prayer they make the vow:

> "I will not cease from mental strife,
>   Nor shall my sword rest in my hand,
>   Till we have built 'Jerusalem'
>   In England's green and lovely land."

BELGIUM AND THE WAR

"They shall not hurt nor destroy in all my holy mountain:
For the earth shall be full of the knowledge of the
Lord, as the waters cover the sea." Isaiah 11:9.

In Byron's day, Italy, with her bleeding heart under the heel of the conqueror and her fairest provinces torn from her helpless hands, was the "Niobe of Nations," so Byron called her, seeing her weeping like the Theban queen, though turned to stone by an angry God for her slaughtered children.

Today Belgium is the "Niobe of Nations." Early this summer there were living in Belgium seven million and a half of the most contented people in Europe. Few of them were millionaires; few of them had what we call "wealth" in America; but they were all industrious and economical and earning each day their daily bread, with prayer, and looking fearlessly into the future.

Today the population of Belgium is a scant three millions. All these last weeks and months every avenue of egress and exit, by land or by sea, has been thronged and choked by masses of men, women and children hurrying into Holland, France or England.

One-third of these remaining three millions are paupers. There are large numbers of people everywhere in Europe, as well as in Belgium, who are living from hand to mouth,

31

but with perfect satisfaction to themselves. Many of these Belgians had, as their entire possessions, a little plot of ground, often less than an acre, or a little shop, and, when ejected from the ground or shop, they were driven from what they looked upon as an earthly paradise, into pauperism as loathsome to them as it would be to us—pauperism so deep, despairing, and hopeless that you and I, perhaps have never seen the like of it.

All this might have been prevented by a scrap of paper with the King's signature upon it, or by a nod of the King's head or a wave of his hand. But these petty farmers, merchants and shopkeepers sided with their sovereign and were ready to lay their country and themselves on the altar of the Ideal. They refused, with all the consequences before their eyes, to join even tacitly in a war in which they had no more interest than we. They threw their little band of soldiers against the most highly trained army, "the best fighting machine," it has been called, in Europe, making a marvelous and altogether incomprehensible resistance.

Driven slowly back, the Belgians saw their fields devastated, their cities like Termonde, Alost, and Dinant, burned; their university town of Louvain, with its beautiful cathedral, destroyed. They saw their capital, Brussels, often compared with Paris, occupied by foreign troops, and their great commercial city, Antwerp, not only occupied, but placed with Brussels under an exhausting and seemingly impossible tribute.

If this be modern war, as we are told it is, if any army—if every army—under like circumstances must commit such deeds as were thought possible only in the dark ages, then war is as subversive of civilization as it is of Christianity.

32

This little kingdom of Belgium has been the shuttle-cock
and football of Europe, knocked and kicked hither and yon
from the time when all there was of it was a semi-civilized
tribe called the Belgae inhabiting its marshes and forests.
To this tribe belonged one of those famous "three parts"
into which Cæsar said "all Gaul is divided." And Cæsar
did his very best to compel those three parts to become a
single Roman province. But those few savage Belgians
had no more hesitation in resisting Cæsar's legions
than their descendants had in resisting "the best fighting
troops in the world." Ever since Cæsar's day Belgium has
been the battlefield of Europe, the "Bowl" in which kings
and emperors have struggled for the goal of continental or
universal supremacy. Whoever conquered, Belgium lost
and was tossed with the rest of the loot to the victor. She
belonged in rapid succession to Austria, France, Spain, and
Holland.

Not only did Julius Cæsar fight his first recorded battle
in Belgium, but there also King Clovis met and conquered
his foes. There the Saracens, it is said, were hurrying
when the blow of Charles Martel's hammer near Poitiers
staggered and stopped them. There, most terrible of all the
events in Belgium's tragic history till the wave of this war
swept over her, came an army of the cruelest soldiers, as
they were reputed, in Europe, under the leadership of the
Duke of Alva. To speak Alva's name today in the ears of
Belgians or of Hollanders is to bring up before the eyes of
those who hear a vision of a monster of inhumanity.

In a single year, it is said, 75,000 persons were put to
death by Alva and his soldiers. For the most part they
were non-combatants and the only crime that was charged
against them was that they were patriotic or that they were

Protestants or that they were possessed of treasure desired by Alva or his minions.

In 1568 Antwerp was called the wealthiest city in Europe. She possessed at least 500 marble mansions, for the records prove that in that year 500 mansions of marble were destroyed in the so-called "Spanish Fury." You may read the story of it in "The Rise of the Dutch Republic," by our own Motley, but if you have not a heart of iron you cannot read it without tears.

For three days the city was sacked by Spanish soldiers, who were given full license to do as they liked with the persons and the property of the inhabitants. That 8,000 men, women and children were massacred in those three days is the least terrible part of the story. From the infant just born to the octogenarian, without discrimination of sex, all alike suffered inconceivable and unspeakable tortures in this debauch of demons. The pavements of the churches, to which crowds had fled for safety, were piled high with corpses and the narrow streets were impassable with the wounded, the dying and the dead. Compared with the devastation wrought in this pandemonium, all that happened in two invasions by the emissaries of Louis XIV, and in the English invasion of Marlborough, the emissary of Queen Anne and the despotic Sarah Churchill and the final desperate and despairing struggle of Napoleon at Waterloo but a few miles from Brussels for the throne of the world, were of trifling importance.

The prosperity of modern Belgium, since her neutrality was guaranteed in 1839 by England, France, Austria, Russia and Prussia, is not by any means due to the extent of her territory, for Belgium is only a little triangle between France, Germany, Holland and the sea. That triangle is but 165 miles long and 120 miles broad, containing 11,400 square miles. It is about the same size as two of our rather diminutive States, Rhode Island and Connecticut, with a fair-sized State like Massachusetts thrown in. Belgium has, it is true, 900,000 square miles of territory in the Congo, but, at present, they are almost negligible.

Neither has Belgium enormous mineral wealth like our Nevada, Colorado and California. She has a belt of coal and iron coming up out of northwestern France, which gives her a value altogether disproportionate to her size For coal and iron in Europe will soon be seemingly of greater value than silver and gold, for you cannot make cannon or warships out of the so-called "precious metals." This iron of Belgium is the "hematite" or blood-red iron, and is considered essential for fine tools and weapons of war.

But Belgium's real wealth comes, not out of the bowels of the earth, but from the surface, from her Lilliputian farms.

We have in our northwest what we call wheat lands; great plains, boundless, shimmering under the sun, palpitating with the heat of the long summer, and from those plains our farmers succeed in raising, on the average, fifteen bushels to the acre. The Belgians, with their little holdings, raise twice that, and then seven extra bushels tossed in for good measure. With Belgium's productivity our single State of Texas could find place and provisions for the whole population of Europe, and all our States together, if equally well cultivated, could support the entire population of the planet. The Belgians are not the most highly educated people in Europe, but they were the first to have public schools, though these schools were intended almost entirely for boys.

It means very much to Belgium that, in her picturesque and musty town of Ghent, the greatest of Spanish kings and German emperors, Charles V, was born. But it means a great deal more to us Americans that on the 24th of December, 1814, in that same town of Ghent, a treaty of peace was signed between the United States and Great Britain. More significant still, that treaty has been kept to this hour. It is not necessarily true that treaties are made only to be broken in a great crisis. Wherever the high contracting parties take as their cry, not "dominion or death," but the slogan of the French Republic reversed— not "liberty, equality, fraternity"—but "fraternity, equality, liberty"—then solemn promises, though made by nations, will be solemnly observed.

Well would it be for these warring potentates of Europe if they might, on the 24th day of this December, journey to that sleepy little town of Ghent, "where it is always afternoon," and, standing together before that house in which Charles V was born, recall his life, with its unrivaled power, pomp and splendor, and remember that there came a day when, possessing all that they are fighting for and more, he laid down the mightiest scepter a human hand ever held for the staff of a penitent monk. "So passes away the glory of the world."

While the Belgians are proud of Charles V, they are not nearly so proud of him as conqueror or penitent monk as they are of their painter, Rubens. Rubens, it is true, was not born in Belgium, but he spent most of his life in Antwerp and did his best work there. His two greatest pictures, "The Elevation on the Cross" and "The Descent from the Cross," are hanging, or were hanging till a few weeks ago, in the Antwerp Cathedral.

Out of a dispute over a plot of ground came the first of these paintings. Surely there has been no plot of ground in Belgium, or in all Europe, that has been more productive. No quarrel before or since has resulted in so much good to the world.

Symbolic to Belgium eyes must "The Elevation on the Cross" have seemed during these weeks in which Belgium, herself, was being lifted up upon the cross of sorrow by hands as hard as those of the Roman soldiers. But if Belgium should ever come to see that as Jesus, our Lord, hung upon His cross that He might conquer the enmity of man, and beat down forever that great serpent, Satan, beneath his feet—so she, by her sorrows, has had a part in putting an end to strife between nations, then, indeed, may she feel that some, at least, of her griefs have been gains. All persons or peoples who go to the cross rather than surrender truth and righteousness and honor are crucified with Christ.

Intensely as we disapprove of the treatment that the Congo Free States were reported—doubtless with too much truth—to have received at the hands of Leopold II, we are not prepared to believe that because the people of the Congo were tortured by a luxurious and lecherous king to increase revenues which he squandered on his favorites—that therefore the innocent people of Belgium, many of whom have never even heard of the Congo, are being crushed beneath the horrors of this war.

That would be a kind of rudimentary justice which satisfies the heart of a savage and the hearts of some who are semi-civilized as well. But it was against just that sort of justice that our Lord made his protest. When the Pharisees came to Jesus and said, "Who did sin?"—as they pointed to the blind man, they were not thinking of hygienic, but of ethical sin, of transgression of God's holy law—"Who did sin, this man or his parents?"—"somebody must have sinned, for this is plainly the penalty." And Jesus said, "Nobody; this is an act of God and you are not ready yet for the full explanation of it." "Thou knowest not now; thou shalt know hereafter." So, too, when they came to Him and asked about the eighteen men who were trapped under the falling stones and timbers of the tower of Siloam, what particular sin they had committed, Jesus made the same reply. They were sinners, of course, as all men are, but they were not particular sinners who needed to be particularly punished in just that particular way.

Unless a man has the inspiration of the old Hebrew prophets, he dare not say that Belgium is suffering now for the sins of Leopold II. But you and I can say that Belgium is suffering for her situation. Neither would we dare say that England is suffering because there have been Englishmen who may have made large fortunes by the sale of opium; or that France is suffering because there may have been Frenchmen who ground down the natives of Madagascar for gold; or that Germany is suffering because there may have been Germans who have enslaved both white men and black men in order to grow rich rapidly. But they all are suffering the agonies of this war, because they have all alike, though in varying degrees, refused to seek first the Kingdom of God and His righteousness. They are not fighting in Europe tonight because Christianity has failed, but because these warring Kings and emperors have failed in living up to the Christianity which they have professed.

Do you doubt that, if a decade ago the nations of Europe had adopted the Golden Rule as final, there would be peace in Europe now? Do you doubt that if, at the close of this war, all rulers shall honestly and sincerely adopt that Rule as the last word concerning the relation, not only of man to man, but of nation to nation, that peace will be permanent? Then shall dawn that day the Prophet foresaw "When they shall not hurt nor destroy in all God's holy mountain, for the earth shall be full of the knowledge of the Lord as the waters cover the sea."

Our pity has gone out toward Belgium in a great throb of desire that, so far as possible, we might undo that which has been done. If our hearts have, indeed, been harrowed, then out of the furrow should come not only pity, but piety. Only piety can protect pity from the winds that level it to the earth and from the sun that scorches and shrivels it. If the pity that you and I have for Belgium meets with piety, if piety and pity blend in our breasts, then shall we find ourselves not only pitying our poor brothers of Belgium, but we shall be moved with a piety which will enable us to pray even for those whose hands are as stained with innocent blood as the hands of the men who elevated the Christ on His cross: "Father, forgive them; for they know not what they do."

FRANCE AND THE WAR

"Let the beauty of the Lord our God be upon us." Psalm
90:17.

What the golden spike in the center of the Roman Forum,
serving as the last of the milestones, was to the Roman
Empire, the Egyptian obelisk in the center of the Place de
la Concorde in Paris is to France. This square is not only
the most majestic, splendid, and beautiful in Europe, but,
with the single exception, possibly, of the Roman Forum, it
is the most suggestive historically. Here in epitome and
microcosm is the history of the country that for three centuries swayed the destiny and shaped the literature and
language, the life and character of every province in
Europe.

Standing by the side of that obelisk on the spot where,
in a few months in the years 1793 and 1794, Louis XVI
and his beautiful queen, Marie Antoinette, and, 2,800 supposed aristocrats were guillotined, the eye is caught by the
glitter of the great statues on the colossal bridge of Alexander III, symbolic of the alliance between France and the
Giant of the North—an offering supposed to have closed
the chasm made by the Crimean War.

Just beyond, across the Seine, are the pillared porticos
of the Chamber of Deputies—the French Parliament. It

is a far call from the France of today, the only great power in Europe that has not even the fiction, much less the fact, of a king, to the "imperial imposter," as Victor Hugo brands him, who cajoled and coerced France for more than two decades. Victor Hugo's "History of a Crime," as he calls the Coup d'Etat, is as brilliant as it is blasting. He tells this story of this "nephew of his uncle," President of France, who, by duplicity and violence, succeeded in making himself and his family heirs forever of the Empire, so he believed. Twenty years later the sun, not of "Austerlitz," set to rise no more.

To the left is the glittering dome of Les Invalides, established by Napoleon I as the home of his old soldiers, like our Old Soldiers' Home, of which we have good reason to be proud. Napoleon said: "I found the crown of France lying in the dust, and I picked it up on the point of my sword." It was a great crown; a crown that had encircled the head of Charlemagne—Charles the Great—but it was not great enough for the little head of the little corporal from Corsica.

So he began to collect in rapid succession all the crowns of Europe. The iron crown of Italy, the jeweled crown of Austria, and the Holy Roman Empire; the golden chaplet of the Hohenzollerns, and all the lesser crowns of the lesser kings of Bavaria, Wurtemburg, Saxony, Holland, and Spain. But there were two crowns he could not get. The crown of England and the crown of Russia and for these two crowns he was quite willing to give all the rest.

With kings as his captains and aides-de-camp he marched away at the head of the grandest army the world had thus far seen, of 550,000 veterans. In the Kremlin, at Moscow, he found one of the crowns he sought; the crown that had been worn by Catherine the Great, and by Peter the Great, and almost in that same hour he read his doom, written with letters of fire on the sky and with snow and ice on streets and fields, on pinnacles and spires.

He was conquered, the Russians say, by "the three greatest military leaders the world knows anything about: General Frost, General Famine" and then, as we might expect, the Russians add the name of their own general, "General Kutusoff."

Cowering in the cushions of his carriage, Napoleon crossed the borders into France, leaving, apparently, without a thought, all that remained of the great army to die amid the snows and the storms of the Russian steppes. Slowly before him, though he saw it not, "the sun of Waterloo" was rising and, far out in the Atlantic, a little island was being made ready for his coming. A broken-hearted and saddened prisoner, dying at St. Helena, he said: "Bury me on the banks of the Seine amid the people I have loved so well." Amid the people, two million of whose sons—the tallest, the strongest, the bravest, the most efficient—he had led out to slaughter. When once the love of glory crazes a man, is there any room left in his heart for any love—save the love of self?

Looking north, a Greek temple, called now the Church of the Madelaine, closes a short boulevard. Napoleon intended to make that temple another monument to his own glory, as he intended to make the whole world a temple for the same object. But a day is coming, if we pray and work for it, when all the temples of glory, columns of victory and arches of triumph, shall be consecrated to the glory of God.

On the right is a vast section that was once covered by the Tuilleries, or the "brickyards," as the word means. There stood, till they were burned by the Commune in 1871, the palaces of the French kings and emperors. Immediately adjacent, still in its perfectness, is the incomparable art gallery of the Louvre, once part of the imperial palaces. It is the center of French art and of artistic France.

As Germany suggests efficiency, military and mechanical; as England suggests democracy, in spite of the monarchy which is a fiction, and a House of Lords which is a tradition, and a State Church which is an anachronism—like that of Scotland—as all the vital institutions of England are essentially democratic, leading on inevitably to a government of the people, for the people, and by the people—so France suggests aesthetic refinement and artistic skill. The French have not always, it is true, prayed that "the beauty of the Lord, their God, might be upon them." They have not always loved the true and the good as they have loved the beautiful. But they have at least tried to be thus far, godlike, that they have attempted "to make all things beautiful in their time." Beautiful buildings, beautiful squares, beautiful streets, beautiful bridges, beautiful furniture, down to the key with which not less artistic locks are opened, are all wrought "with greatest care" "as in the earlier days of art," of which Longfellow sings.

France has the trick, so her enemies call it, of the transforming hand. By her touch she does what life does by its touch. Life touches the seed in the soil and transforms it upward. Fire touches the tree and transforms it downward. France takes all that is material and coarse and ugly and transforms it into beauty.

The French artist, Millet, so one of our American critics says, spent fifty cents for a canvas, and twenty-five cents

44

more for some tubes of paint, and with color and genius changed the cotton into "The Angelus" for which, even in France, where they consider values very carefully, they were willing to pay $107,000 and for which, when the plutocratic Americans came in and began to bid, the price soon ran up to $250,000. Far better than the touch of Midas, that transforms sticks and stones into gold, is the touch of the skilled French hand which transforms ugliness into beauty.

From one of the windows of the Louvre you look out on a mounted statue, impressive because of pose, vivacity and force, and still more because it is the face of a woman that gazes from the open visor. Five hundred years ago, on the 6th of January, 1412, a child was born in a peasant's house at Domrémy, not far from the Vosges Mountains. That child became, if not the most famous woman in the world—and that may well be asserted—certainly the most remarkable. Where is there a page of history that is comparable for its incredibleness, its incomprehensibleness, its heroism and its pathos, with the page that tells the story of Jeanne d'Arc, the Maid of Domrémy?

While she was watching the sheep, the Archangel Michael appeared to her, so she thought. He told her that the time had come when she was to be the flail with which God would drive the English out of France. Her Father and mother were pious peasants and naturally superstitious. They believed her story. After much effort, and after bringing forward what seemed to be incontestable proofs, she persuaded some of the nobles of France that she had seen these visions. At last she won over the weak, vacillating, treacherous king, Charles VII. In three months she had conquered the bravest of the English captains commanding armies that never before had known anything but victory.

Blood is said to be thicker than water. If you have English blood you may hesitate to applaud her conquest, but wherever there is an invader, wherever there is a despoiler, let him come with what flag he will, American hearts will rejoice when that flag trails in the dust. In four months Jeanne d'Arc led the French army into the old French city of Rheims—today, alas, ruined by war. There the king was crowned, and crowned, in fact, by the hand of the maid of Domrémy. Her soldiers had begun to believe, as half France now believes, that if she were not altogether an angel, she was something more than human. One of the old chroniclers, in his frank, blunt way of speaking, says of her—"A thing wholly divine whether to see or hear."

From the last scene in her life every Englishman may well turn away his face in shame. Caught at last treacherously by the English soldiers, she was condemned by the English captain to be burned in the square at Rouen. "She was a sorceress," they said, and she was. By such sorcery any nation today might be saved. When the fire reached her flesh her head sank on her breast and she gave but one cry, "Jesus." As the crowd broke up, an English soldier muttered: "We are lost, for we have burned a saint."

Passing down the Rue de Rivoli, under the windows of the Louvre, you come at last to the open door from which the Empress Eugenie, with but one companion, made her escape from the infuriated crowds that had even then begun to burn her palace of the Tuilleries. She found her way to the home of an American dentist, where she was concealed, till later on, by his ingenuity, she succeeded in making her escape to England.

Just opposite that door is a little church called St.-Germain-l'Auxerrois, and from its dark belfrey, on the 24th of August, 1572, the signal was given for one of the most monstrous crimes ever enacted upon this earth. From one of the windows of the Louvre the young king, Charles IX, who was a mere tool in the hands of his terrible mother, Catherine de Medici, fired a pistol shot as the sign, and the bells were rung and the massacre began. That night in Paris five thousand of the cleanest, whitest souls Paris ever saw, among them Admiral Coligny, were slaughtered; and in the provinces seventy thousand more shared their fate. That was the most dramatically tragic incident in the history of Protestantism in France, but it was by no means the most fatal hour in that history.

When Protestantism first came to France it came, of course, from Germany. Let us ever gratefully remember that the greatest reform the world has yet known began with a German monk in Wittenberg.

At its coming the French Court was pleasantly interested. Francis I was a most intelligent king. His buildings are still one of the wonders of France. His sister, Margaret of Navarre, was quite as intelligent. They were fascinated, as Guizot says, "by the genius of Erasmus, the sharp satire of Hutton, and by Luther's weighty tractates." Forty-six years after Luther nailed his theses to the door of the church in Wittenberg, a French Cardinal wrote to the Pope in a perfect terror of anticipation: "The kingdom is already half Protestant."

But as Protestantism came to be better understood; as the Court saw that it was not merely an intellectual renaissance, a protest against the vulgarity, superstition and cupidity of the monks; but that it was aimed at corruption and immorality—even in kings' houses—it did not seem quite so attractive. The French king came to feel about it very much as the Roman emperors felt about Christianity, when they saw how revolutionary it was. They were right in saying: "There is not room enough in our Empire for a religion like this and for a government like ours." So the French court turned against Protestantism, and Protestantism was not guiltless—too much reliance was put upon force and political influence. Great names were on the church rolls—names like those of the Prince de Condé and Admiral Coligny. Some of the noblest families in France were Protestant. They trusted in their rank and position. "If they dare persecute us, we are not unwilling to test our strength with theirs."

So Protestantism fought seven wars. Not riots, not rebellions, but counted in the chronicles of France as wars. Seven wars, in not one of which was Protestantism defeated. They all ended in treaties honorable, it was believed, to both parties.

Where force had failed, subtlety might succeed: "Let us be brethren," the Romanists said, "and live in peace." "Let us bring together these two religions that are not so different, by a royal marriage." "Here is your Protestant, Henry; let him espouse our Margaret of Valois, and henceforth we two shall be one." The Protestants were wild with joy. They thought henceforth the sheep would be securely guarded by the wolf. They hurried to Paris. Thousands of them were within the walls of the city when the bell of St.-Germain rang out for the marriage celebration, soon to be sealed in the blood of St. Bartholomew's Day.

When Philip of Spain, who was contemplating an Armada to be sent against England, heard of the massacre, he gave one great guffaw—the only time in all his life, it is said, when anyone heard him laugh—and, alas, when the Pope of Rome heard of it, he did not cover himself with sackcloth and ashes, but smiled and commanded a Te Deum speedily to be sung. That Te Deum has died away, but, unfortunately for the Pope, he ordered a medal to be struck in commemoration of "the glorious hour." That medal you may see today in the Vatican.

In 1598 was issued the so-called "Edict of Nantes," a little town of France that never would have been remembered but for that event. This edict gave complete religious liberty to all the Protestants of France. But Louis XIV and Madame de Maintenon had the idea—and it is not a modern idea by any means—that treaties are very elastic, and they began immediately, as Guizot says, to deal with Protestantism as a serpent deals with its proposed victim.

Madame de Maintenon wrote: "We will speedily make it quite ridiculous to be of this religion." It was soon much more serious than that. When the Edict of Nantes was revoked in 1685 by Louis, at Madam de Maintenon's suggestion, France became a great hospital. All the artisans, all the skilled workmen and manufacturers seemed to have been permeated by this so-called heresy, and, when they understood what the edict meant, they began to flee in every direction from France, as thousands have been fleeing for the last few months from Belgium. Fenelon wrote: "France has been impoverished of more than a million men." What kind of men they were you can see when you look to England and Holland, to Germany and to the United States. Wherever you find the Huguenot, or the descendant of the Huguenot, there you find a man with clear spiritual vision, cunning hand, and true conscience—a soldier of Christ.

France has never recovered from that colossal crime, that prodigious error, that incredible blunder. The revolution of 1793 was the legitimate child of that act of Louis and Madame de Maintenon. The French people had been taught that it was right, under certain circumstances, to lift their hands against their brethren. France had lost in their eyes the mother's heart. When the proletariat rose against the throne in 1793, and the secularists against the church in 1903, France was simply reaping what she had sown. She had trampled her best religious blood in the mire. The religious talent was not extirpated by disuse, but it was almost smothered under secularism and sensuality.

But when the Scot, Robert W. McAll, went to Paris, just after the Commune, he did not believe that religion had died out of the French heart. His biographer says: "He always had a way of finding flowers where no one else believed there were any, and sometimes in passing a seemingly flowerless copse he would say, 'It looks to me as though there might be white hyacinths there,' and, lo, in a few minutes, behold them." He believed, even in Belleville, that flowerless copse of Paris, that home of anarchy, that though he could not hope to find there "the white flower of a sinless life," he might find the red flower of remorse and repentance.

"What France needs," said someone, "is not a man"—France has always been a hero-worshiper—"What France needs is not a man, but a God." When McAll told them about God, the Father of our Lord, Jesus Christ, the God manifest in the flesh, Himself a working man, these *ouvriers,* these working men of Belleville, and of all the other villes of France crowded into his halls until there was scarcely a town where there was not such a hall for the preaching of the gospel. Auxiliaries, too, were established in England, Scotland, and in America. One of those auxiliaries we have here in Washington.

Since 1871, when France was brought to her knees by her terrible defeat, the French heart has softened. Her great authors, like Brunetière, and Bourget, and Francois Coppée, have become the prophets of the new order. They have cried out against the frivolity—against the lubricity of France. The greatest of her modern philosophers, Bergson, from his high peak, looking down, not only over France, but over the whole world, has told France that the greatest treasure she has is not her skilled hands, nor her trained eye, but the Life in her soul. Like an old Hebrew prophet, he sees a vision of vastness. "All the living hold together, and all yield to the same tremendous push. The animal takes its stand on the plant. Life in man bestrides animality, the whole of humanity in space and time is an immense army galloping beside and before and behind each of us, and overcoming all obstacles; in an overwhelming charge able to beat down every resistance and clear the most formidable obstacles, perhaps even death."

We have our bursts of generous feeling toward France. Whenever we are compelled to recall or whenever we voluntarily recall the days that followed 1776 we honestly say to ourselves: "If it had not been for Lafayette and Rochambeau; if it had not been for the men and the ships and the money that France sent us—we do not know!" But far better than to build, as we have occasionally, a monument to some French Revolutionary hero here in American cities,

51

is what we have done in Paris. There we have erected a Young Men's Christian Association—a well-equipped edifice built by the generosity of an American citizen. In addition—it is a short story; far too short—we have sent to France the most perfectly equipped modern hospital and ambulance corps, it is said, in the world; a hospital in which there are skilled surgeons who are able to heal wounds and to graft bones. They transpose not only the bones from the hand or the leg of a man, but they take a bone from the hand or the leg of another man and compel it to grow. In this hospital bacteria of all sorts find their occupation gone. Here, too, there are American dentists, incomparably the best in the world, ready to treat the teeth of wounded soldiers. They have come to understand in France and elsewhere in Europe that a soldier is no better than his teeth.

We have spent a great deal of money, we Americans, in Paris and in France, but we have spent most of that money for our own people. It is sometimes cynically asked "whether Americans still go to Paris when they die." Without attempting to answer a question of that sort, we are at least safe in saying that many Americans go to Paris while they live. As in olden times multitudes were drawn to Rome, in the time of her glory; and to Florence in the days of Lorenzo the Magnificent—so now they are drawn to Paris. Drawn by her great universities, drawn still more by her technical schools of art and of music, of science and of invention.

There were before the war broke out more than 3,000 American students in Paris. For the Americans living in Paris we have built three churches and two social clubs —one for men, the other for women—and a Sunday Evening Club, of which the one that meets in Orchestra Hall in Chicago is the child. Since 1895, when the "Students' Atelier Reunions" were organized, some four hundred students have gathered every Sunday night in one of the halls of Paris to listen to good music—there is no better in Paris, some of the finest artists there are always ready to volunteer their services for these meetings. They listen to good music, they listen to good sermons, and they have good cheer. From the first, an American clergyman has been in charge of this work devoting his whole time to these students. Now that many of the students will be away necessarily from Paris while the war lasts, the attention of the minister in charge is given largely to the relief of the innumerable refugees from Belgium and the provinces.

Turning once more, we look to the west to a great triumphal arch, far more splendid than the triumphal arch of Titus, at Rome. Underneath that arch and down the Champs Elysées, a boulevard five times as broad as our boasted Pennsylvania Avenue, there marched in 1871 the German army with the newly-crowned emperor at its head. That scene is burned into the heart and soul of France, and the strips of flesh—the two provinces of Alsace and Lorraine—which were then torn from her and joined to the German Empire, still bleed—the wounds of war close slowly—War "makes a solitude and calls it peace."

France, they say, is fighting to get back those provinces; fighting for revenge—"La Revanche"—but no one has charged France yet with having begun the war. This hydra-headed war seems to have had as many births as it has heads. It was born, it is said, in Servia, in Austria, in Germany, in Russia, in England, in the Balkans; it was born, they say now, in 1878, in Bulgaria, at the time of the

Bulgarian massacre—but no one yet has said that it was born in France. The hand that threw open the doors of the Temple of Janus—was not a French hand.

France is the father of the Crusades. The word *croisade* is French and shows the origin of the movement itself. Guizot tells the story of Peter Gautier, of Amiens, and his journey to the Holy Land. The officer became a pilgrim. When he recounted to Pope Urban II the story of what he had seen in Jerusalem, of the sacrilege committed at sacred places, he was given an edict permitting him to call all Europe to war. Kings, nobles and knights seized their swords, mounted their steeds and rode toward the Holy Land to deliver the tomb of their Lord from the hands of the heathen.

France needs today to father a new crusade, for which she is pre-eminently fitted—a crusade against the primeval forests of Science, uncharted and unconquered. From such a crusade some of her soldiers have come already bringing precious treasure. Two of them returned with radium. Another brought the antiseptic treatment of wounds by which thousands of lives have been saved. These are treasures far greater than those for which, as well as for his Lord's tomb, the Crusader risked his life.

France is pre-eminently fitted by the clearness of her vision, by the penetration with which she sees into "the permanent forces," to become the leader of a crusade which shall call out all her powers. A crusade against ignorance and disease; a crusade for humanity, morality and righteousness. Then shall France see the beauty of the Lord, her God, descending upon her, and Paris shall become religiously, as well as æsthetically and socially, the Capital of the World.

RUSSIA AND THE WAR

———

Blessed is the nation whose God is the Lord."   Psalm
  33:12.

———

In the Scandinavian legend the god, Thor, found the
giant, Skimir, whom he particularly disliked, sound asleep.
He lifted the famous hammer, with which he had often
crushed mountains, and struck the giant a terrific blow.
Skimir turned uneasily in his sleep, rubbed his forehead,
and said: "Did a fly bite me?"   Then Thor pulled himself
together for a more tremendous effort, and Skimir
moved, evidently in pain, muttering: "Did a bee sting me?"
Thor, in disgust, turned away from a giant who was too
stupid to know when his skull was cracked!

Russia, whom all the world nowadays is calling "The
Colossus of the North," bestrides not two islands, like her
namesake of Rhodes, but two continents.   Struck hard,
"She does not sulk, she meditates," says Gortschakoff.
When she grows uneasy, she merely shifts the center of
gravity from Asia to Europe or from Europe to Asia, till
a continent seems to tilt.   Russia is so vast that when you
take a map of Europe and Asia and look at it hurriedly it
seems as if there were little else upon it.   Great Britain,
France, Spain, Austria, Germany, Italy, and the Balkans,
all combined, are not so great as European Russia.   When
we measure ourselves against her, her 2,100,000 square
miles in Europe seem small compared with our 3,600,000

square miles. But when Asiatic Russia lifts up its head, with its 6,700,000 square miles, we are almost lost to sight.

Russia, it is said, could cut ten corn states like ours from the black earth belt north of the Himalayas, and twelve wheat states equal to the wheat-growing states of the United States and Canada. We built our greatest railroad 3,000 miles from ocean to ocean. But some American travelers crossing Siberia, after traveling for three days, found it necessary, in order to secure permission for the conductor to turn on the steam in the car in which they were riding, to telegraph 6,000 miles to St. Petersburg—the next day, when it grew warmer, they were obliged to telegraph again to St. Petersburg for permission to have the steam turned off.

In this vast country there are one hundred and seventy millions of people—almost twice the population of America. Is this Russia a monster, a menace to civilization, or is she a messenger of courage, of hope, of a larger and better liberty? The answer means much to us for Russia is our nearest neighbor among the great European powers. Canada lies on our borders, it is true, but Canada is a colony of England, while Siberia, an imperial province of Russia, is only forty miles from Alaska. A railroad has been talked of from Washington to Petrograd without change of cars.

Consider first the Russianizing of Russia: How she came to find herself. It is not an historical romance, but it is a romance of history.

There came, no one knows exactly whence, but probably from some part of Sweden, three princes of Rus, of whom the best known to fame is Rurik, the eldest. They were invited, it is said, by the tribes living along the headwaters of the Dnieper, who were fighting among themselves, and, apparently, as in Mexico, it was to be a fight to the finish without intervention. Such an opportunity was not to be refused. The Rus princes were so successful that in a comparatively short time they succeeded in making themselves supreme in all the provinces.

Their first capital was Kieff, and their first great conquest, outside their own country, was Constantinople. Constantinople did not surrender to them, but the great city was so badly frightened that the Greek Emperor gave his sister as consort to Vladimir I on condition that Vladimir and his people should accept Christianity. So Christianity came into Russia from Constantinople. It was therefore what is called the Orthodox Greek Church. Today the largest body of Greek Christians in the world is in Russia.

But the Russianizing of Russia was hastened by the Tartars or Mongolians. In 1238 they came from the east like locusts out of the air. "For our sins," one old Russian chronicler has written, "unknown nations arrived. No one knew their origin, whence they came or what religion they practiced." Then was first heard the name, the terrible name, of Genghis Khan, the tyrant and despot of Mongolia and China, the walls of whose capital, men believed, were built of the skulls of his enemies. For three centuries the Russian princes paid tribute to their Mongolian masters; but, at the first sign of weakness, as might have been expected, they rose unitedly and broke the yoke. So Russia was Russianized into the Tsardom of Muscovy. Three men, Ivan III the Great, his son Basil and his grandson, Ivan IV, stand out against the sky line.

The second stage, The Unification of Russia, was not difficult for men of that type. Just as it is no trouble for a boa constrictor to unify a goat, a sheep, a calf; if it can once get itself around them and crush their bones. Ivan III, Basil and Ivan IV were remarkably successful in the boa constrictor class. They encircled the Russian princes, crushed their bones and assimilated them. When Novgorod, one of the independent principalities, resisted, Ivan the Terrible—he was well named—visited them for six weeks, during which time he tore out the tongues of all his critics, and put to death 60,000 men, women and children. The unification of Novgorod was complete.

The Europeanizing of Russia, the third stage, was begun by Peter the Great. When Peter was a boy in the royal palace it seemed very probable that he would never be heard from. That was the hope of his aunt, Sophia, who was the regent, and who very earnestly, as she confessed, plotted his assassination. If Peter had been anything but the son of a Czar he would have run away from Russia and become a sailor. As it was he walked deliberately away from Russia and became a royal tramp and the most famous of Czars. For a year and a half in Holland, in England, in Germany, and in Austria, he went everywhere, and with those wonderful eyes of his he saw everything, and with those wonderful hands of his he could make anything he had seen. In the shipyards in Holland he began the Russian Navy.

When he returned from his wanderings he was fully equipped for the Europeanizing of Russia. He built what he called "a window out of which Russia might look upon Europe." On the banks of the Neva, in the marshes, he drove great beams upon which he erected palaces and homes for princes and people who were not yet there. But there were no houses to let very long in St. Petersburg.

Peter issued a royal edict that 100,000 nobles, mechanics, merchants and doctors should come to St. Petersburg and stay there. They refused at the peril of their lives. In this great city, great from the beginning, there were no lawyers. While Peter was in England he stood one day near Westminster Hall and saw a procession entering the law courts. He asked who the men in the big wigs were. "Lawyers," was the answer. He counted them and said: "There are twenty. Have you got twenty lawyers in this little England?" When they said "Yes," he replied, in surprise: "I have but two in Russia, and as soon as I get back I am going to behead one of them."

He was a radical reformer, as you may see. He not only shaved his own beard, which was considered heresy of the extremest sort in Russia—it was marring the image of God—but he compelled all his courtiers to shave theirs, which was as great an offense as it would be if the present Czar should compel his court ladies to shave their heads. He was not satisfied merely with being an imperial barber, he made himself an imperial dentist as well. He took three of his courtiers, one day, seated them in a chair and filled their teeth, that they might know how it should be done. Neither did his imperial consort escape from his paternalism. When he had heard on his travels that something had been done in the palace by her dictation or her permission, which he disliked, he wrote to her: "I dearly love thee, but on my return I will dust thy jacket well." Yet it was due to this tyrant that Russia was Europeanized.

The work he began was carried on even more rapidly, for everything had been prepared for her by Catherine the Great, who, it is said, robbed all the philosophers of Europe for the benefit of Russia.

Then came Alexander I, one of the Europeanizers, and after him a reactionary brother, Nicholas, who saw the tendencies of things, and said: "My successor may make these changes, but I cannot." It was a pathetic confession of a reactionary. His successor did make the changes.

The fourth stage, which we may call The Modernizing of Russia, began with Alexander II. He emancipated the serfs, an act as great in its courage and wide influence as the emancipation of our slaves by Abraham Lincoln. He emancipated the Press, as far as that was possible in Russia. He called to his aid the very profession so detested by Peter the Great. He had lawyers brought to St. Petersburg, not only from Russia but from every country in Europe, and reorganized the courts, which had been most corrupt, on the French system.

But the Russian people had had a taste of modernism, and they wanted much more and right away.

Alexander felt he was going fast enough, but the modernizers 'organized secret societies all over Russia, among the educated people and the students in the universities, until Russia was practically honeycombed with socialistic and nihilistic organizations. Then, alas, came the fatal error. In 1881, on the 13th of March, when Alexander II was returning to the Winter Palace from a review of a military parade, the revolutionists flung their bombs beneath his carriage. By the first bomb he was badly wounded. He stepped to the pavement to see if anyone else was hurt. Then they threw the second bomb at his feet. He was carried into the palace and died in a little room very modestly furnished, where, upon the writing desk, was a decree granting practically everything that the socialists had asked for, and which he intended to sign that very evening. They who rely on force, on assassination, even though they may think the removal of so-called tyrants is justifiable, are drawing a sword with which they may pierce their own hearts.

After Alexander II came, of course, as we should have expected, a reactionary, Alexander III, who was frightened whenever he remembered the fate of his father. He left the laws that his father had made upon the statute books, but in "innocuous desuetude." There were no reforms, there was no modernizing of Russia under Alexander III.

The present Czar, his son, Nicholas II, favors his father, rather than his grandfather. Yet, during the reign of Nicholas Russia has grown more modern, not rapidly, but steadily. This war, which means so much, which may mean life or death for some of the great nations of Europe, has thus far meant for Russia a completer modernization. The war has done, in a few months, what could have been accomplished, seemingly, only in long years of peace. It has scorched and consumed, in places, the scaffolding, unsightly and constricting, built up around the Russian Empire by bureaucrats till we can see, at least in spots, the structure itself. Russia is not the Czar. The autocrat of all the Russias cannot say, even if he would, with Louis XIV: "I am the state."

Neither is Russia a Church, a mediæval and unreformed Church; nor is it a tangled and entangling system in which machine-like officials attempt perfunctorily to enforce laws as mechanical and irrational as the laws of the Medes and Persians. Russia means one hundred and seventy millions —"mostly barbarians"—so some of our friends who know little about Russia and the Russians are saying.

61

The Russians are the most remarkable people in the world. They are a primitive and primeval people, like their vast woods and their limitless plains. You may hear, in the deep guttural of their tongue, the soughing winds that come from the forests, and across the vast steppes, and you may see, in their deep, well-like eyes, the light that rises up out of the eternities.

The Russian peasants are illiterate. Millions of them can neither read nor write, and yet our Howells—whom some Americans think the greatest of our writers—certainly one of the most delicate and discriminating—calls Tolstoy "the greatest imaginative writer the world has yet seen." And Tolstoy declares that he learned from these illiterate peasants the meaning of life: That life is not a problem, nor a puzzle; that life is not malign nor ironical. When life is toil and self-sacrifice for others, it is the stuff out of which happiness may be made. Looking the world over, seeking for happiness, Tolstoy found it among the peasants. He tried, with extreme literalness, to live like a peasant.

Suspecting that this philosophy was not original with the peasant, he went back to an old Book he had read years before, and had mostly forgotten long ago; there he found all that the peasant had taught him with far deeper interpretations of life in "The Sermon on the Mount."

If we are tempted to look superciliously upon the Russian peasant, let us remember that he is giving us today some of the best illustrations of great religious truths to be found anywhere in the world. A late writer on Russia tells three illuminating stories. The first is about the Turkomans. In 1881 their capital town of Geok-Tepe was assaulted by Russian soldiers and captured, and for three days given over to pillage, spoil and slaughter. In 1914 these Turkomans raised 150,000 roubles for the purchase of a Red Cross hospital, which they equipped with doctors and nurses, and sent to the Czar.

The Kirghiz of Siberia are Asiatic nomads and Mohammedans. Their strongholds were captured, some of their women and children were slaughtered, and, yet, only a few weeks ago, they shipped to Petrograd 500 of their horses, saying, as they sent them: "These are animals accustomed to privation, that will go long and far with very little food." This represented a large part of the possessions left to them after the Russians had dealt with them, as we have time and time again dealt with our American Indians.

The Armenians had their property sequestered; their churches—some of them—were destroyed; their villages were laid waste; and yet they have sent in the last few months a large contribution for the Red Cross of Russia, and hundreds of their young men have enlisted in the Russian Army. "This is not natural," you say. No; but isn't it Christian, this forgiving spirit of the Russian peasant?

In crossing Siberia, there comes to one a sense of immensity beyond dreams. Bewildered by it, we stopped for half an hour at Irkutsk, and, walking down the street, we saw a regiment of Russian soldiers swiftly marching toward us. As they marched they sang, and in that song there was what students of Russian literature tell us they are finding in all the best modern literature of Russia; what they are finding everywhere in Tolstoy—a sob as from the unfathomed depths of a human soul. Underneath that sob, around and penetrating it, was an indefinable atmosphere, as if all that was most ethereal, profound, divine in humanity was speaking through the chant. Singing a song like that men might march to death unconscious of their wounds and with a smile on their faces.

Russia is being modernized largely by the peasant. A new Russia is being built, with the people as the architect of the state, to be founded on "mutual love and magic kindness." You call it a dream; a fantastic dream. Yes, a dream, like the dream of John when he saw the city of God, descending out of Heaven—that city of God which St. Augustine called all Christendom to build here upon the earth. The corner stone of that new Russia, of that city of God, was laid when the Czar moved, perhaps, by what he saw on earth and by the same celestial voices in his own soul, that urged him in 1898 to call that first conference on behalf of peace at The Hague, issued an edict prohibiting the manufacture, use and sale of vodka, the national drink. By a stroke of the pen, the Czar Nicholas cut away one-third of the revenues of Russia, and, at the same time, added to her resources and her prosperity in a proportion which no arithmetical computation can express. Travelers returning from Russia say: "It is as if spring and summer had come now in mid-winter. The villages have been transformed; there are no longer drunken peasants rolling through the streets to their homes, carrying bottles which were making their wives as bestial as themselves; their children, too, were besotted—forty per cent in some schools suffering from alcoholism, but now they are no longer blear-eyed, sallow-cheeked and thick-tongued. Crime in some of the wards of the great cities has disappeared." No wonder the peasants asked that the temporary prohibition of the Czar might be made permanent.

The Russian officers, following the example of their Czar, have excluded wines of all sorts from their military mess. When Vereshchagin painted his pictures of the Russo-Japanese War there were in the corners of the dining room great buckets—he painted what he saw—filled with bottles of champagne. By order of the censor all these buckets were painted out. Before one of the great battles of that war in one mess ten out of twelve officers were drunk. These drunken officers, for the most part, are dead, and their successors are total abstainers, fit to lead men to victory or death.

Would to God that Protestant Great Britain might follow the example of her Greek ally, and that her King, by command of her Parliament and people, might, at a stroke, destroy an enemy far more threatening to England than the German Army or the German submarines.* A famous Bishop of the English Church cried out a few years ago, "I would rather see England free than sober." His sobriety, it may be, was not to be questioned, but prelatical wisdom certainly, in that cry, struck the bottom hard. No nation can be free that is not sober. If the sobriety of the Russian people shall spread across Siberia, and over Behring Straits, and into Alaska and continental America, we might well, with our gratitude and gold, bridge those Straits as the French have bridged the Seine. They call their bridge "Alexander III." He did nothing for America, very little for humanity; but we might call our bridge "Nicholas II," to whom not even the generation that comes after us would be able to repay the debt of gratitude we should owe.

---

*On April 6th an official announcement was issued in London: "By the King's command no wines or spirits will be consumed in any of His Majesty's houses after today."

TURKEY AND THE WAR

"For thou mayest be no longer steward." Luke 16:2.

The fatal error in religion, that has made the Turkish Empire and all other Mohammedan lands faithless to their God-given stewardship, is putting Resignation in the place of Responsibility. This has honeycombed all ambition and robbed man of every motive that makes for progress. The Moslem stands, looking back to Mohammed and his successors for precedents or commands, but he never looks around to discover possibilities of improving either his own condition or the condition of anyone else.

A sluggish South American, when he is asked to exert himself, may respond with extreme politeness: "Mañana," —tomorrow. But a Mohammedan, while less plausible and promising, has a more effective escape from the disagreeable duty of exerting himself in personal or public reforms and betterments in the single word "Kismet"—fate—that word lifts him to an altitude so lofty that emotion is chilled, desire is frozen, and obligation is put in cold storage.

"Whatever is, is right." This is the philosophy that governs the Moslem's entire life in the minutest detail. Is it a fire? He waits, completely resigned, till it has burned his house down or itself out. "It is the will of Allah." Is it a flood? He will watch it with the same resignation till the waters pass out to sea and the river returns to its old channel. "It is the will of Allah."

Therefore, the Turk does nothing voluntarily for himself or humanity. He does not build bridges. He takes the ford that Allah prepared for him. He does not make roads. He follows a cattle path or the bed of a river. He does not erect hospitals in his cities, but says of himself —he is extremely consistent—as of his wife and of his children. "If it be the will of Allah we shall get well; if it be the will of Allah we shall die." He does not pave the streets of his cities—the city itself is an inconsistency in his creed which he does not stop to explain—but he is consistent in leaving streets in the natural state which is doubtless most pleasing to Allah.

However kindly sympathetic and benevolent such a man may be by nature when he is convinced—and he is always open to such a conviction—that it is the will of Allah that his Christian neighbor, with whom he is on the best of terms, should be removed, his only question is will Allah be most pleased to have him removed with a knife or a gun? Put such a man in the ranks with 50,000 other men of the same sort and creed and you have the kind of an army before which Europe has trembled more than once.

Mohammed, the founder of this religion that controls one-tenth of the world's inhabitants more autocratically than any other religion except Christian Science, was, in the broadest meaning of the word, a seer. Carlyle went so far in his extreme generosity as to give him a place not only among his heroes, but among his prophets. Carlyle thinks that in a world made by God and not the devil it is impossible that quackery and fatuity can be permanently successful. "A false man found a religion?"

he cries. "Why, a false man cannot even build a brick house. If he does not know and know truly the properties of mortar, burnt clay and what else he works in, it is no house that he makes, but a rubbish heap—as, alas, the builders of the first tower of this church found to their cost.

Carlyle will not for a moment consent to say that Mohammed was a conscious imposter. He was a seer, that is, he saw deeply into certain phases of truth. He looked at the great, wide ocean of sand around him and from it came the conception of the illimitable, the infinite. He looked at the stars in their countless numbers and felt, as Napoleon felt, when he waved his hand across the sky and said to his infidel marshals: "Who made all this?" Mohammed did not believe that "all this" had been made by men or by demigods. "God is God;" and the great words thrilled his soul and swayed his whole being. "God is God!" But, alas, he went still further and said: "Mohammed is his prophet." He took a perpetual copyright on the interpretation of God.

The symbol of Mohammedanism, the crescent and the star, is scientifically, psychologically and pathetically perfect. For Mohammed believed that the half is better than the whole. A semi-circle with a single star, rather than a circle in the center of countless constellations in a system of which it was but a part, was naturally his chosen sign.

To Mohammed not only was half a loaf better than no bread, but it was better than all the bread of the whole loaf. To him the Old Testament was better than the Old and New Testaments together. He thought a Moslem not only of more value than all the rest of the world, but of more value alone than he would be with the rest of the world added to him. He believed that the Will is of more importance not only than any other single faculty of man, but of more importance than all the faculties and powers of man—reason, affection and will—under the harmonious sway of a predominant passion like love.

He built, therefore, his great structure on a single virtue, Resignation, and on two vices, Slavery and Polygamy. He promised Paradise to every soldier fighting either to slay or to enslave. He promised his soldiers that if they fell with the sword in their hands they should be caught up by angels and carried into a paradise where they should be served by innumerable slaves and houris. He permitted only four wives here on earth, but there were to be no such restrictions in Paradise. Wine was forbidden the faithful here, but there they should drink until they had satisfied an unquenchable thirst. With a faith like that, a faith so admirably adapted to a limited spirituality, and to an unlimited sensuality, was it any wonder that his soldiers went conquering and to conquer?

Before these Moslem hordes, equipped with the best implements of destruction known to the time, European soldiers offered a feeble resistance.   Moslem armies swept around the shores of the Mediterranean, overrunning all Arabia and Northern Africa, Constantinople, and Greece, overwhelming and extinguishing the finest culture the world had even seen.   Conquering at last Spain itself, they held it for 700 years.   In these Moslem wars, and such as these, it is said that more than 10,000,000 non-Moslems were slaughtered.   But every error—for Carlyle was right no false religion can permanently endure—every error carries its doom in its own bosom. A religion emphasizing

70

but one virtue, Resignation, could make conquests but no converts. Wherever Mohammedanism went it was a marauder and a despoiler. The Janisaries, you say, were the sons of Christian mothers and fathers, but they were torn from the bosoms of their mothers when they were babes and were inoculated with the virus of hate for all Christians, most of all for their own relatives.

A religion founded on one virtue and two vices could not permanently endure. Mohammedanism reached its high water mark when it swept through Spain into France, to the very walls of Tours, where Charles Martel, the Frankish king, struck it a stinging, staggering blow with his Thor-like hammer. Nine hundred years later, beneath the walls of Vienna, John Sobieski, King of Poland, inflicted a still more decisive defeat.

The destroying flood that so long threatened European and Christian civilization slowly receded leaving a detritus of mud and ruins which will not wholly disappear for many centuries.

Spain was the first of all the flooded lands to reappear. Then came Greece and the Balkans. In 1912 it seemed as if there was to be nothing left of Turkey in Europe, yet, thanks to the hot temper and shortsighted selfishness of her enemies, she still holds a little strip around Constantinople. But Asia Minor with her seven churches, some of which were founded by Paul and to all of which John wrote: Tarsus, the birthplace of Paul; Antioch, the place where the disciples were first called Christians; Damascus, where Paul had the heavenly vision to which he was always obedient; Bethlehem, the town of the cradle; Jerusalem, with its sepulchre, and its cross—over all these today the crescent floats.

71

Even in Shelley's time, when the wave was receding much less swiftly than in our own, Shelley, who loved to call himself a skeptic, sang, and a note of faith and hope sounds in his song:

"The moon of Mohammed
Arose and it shall set
While blazoned as on Heaven's immortal noon
The cross leads generations on."

Looking out over the Golden Horn the night Germany declared war against Russia we saw a crescent with one star of glittering silver blazing close to it. Together they seemed to dominate heaven and earth. As we looked we pondered, like Franklin in Independence Hall, in Philadelphia, where the Continental Congress was assembled to form, if possible, a Constitution for the United States. Seeing a sun carved on the back of the chair in which the speaker sat, "I wondered," Franklin said, "as I looked, whether it was a setting or a rising sun, but as I gazed long I felt sure that it was a rising sun, and that it foreboded prosperity for the new union which had just been consummated." So we wondered if the crescent, gleaming threateningly in the sky, was waxing or waning. Convinced that it was waning, we saw in it, not a prophecy, but a symbol of Mohammedanism—the half moon waning to wax no more.

The Turks of the better class in Constantinople have shared this to them bitter conviction since Turkey began the war with Russia. One of the wisest of the Turkish statesmen said, when told the first shot had been fired, "This is the end, our fate is sealed." The voice of the Sheik-Ul-Islam, though it carries much further than that of any Sultan, has not been effective in calling the Mohammedans to a holy war. In vain the prophet's banner has been unfurled. In vain the sacred carpet has been exhibited. In vain the sword of Mohammed II, the Conqueror, with which every Sultan is invested in the great mosque of Eyoub, has been pointed at the infidel's breast. The Mohammedan world is unresponsive. One virtue, Resignation, calls to the Moslem's soul with a louder voice than the blended tones of the Sheik-Ul-Islam and the Sultan. "The lines have fallen to me in pleasant places," the Turk says. "I love Constantinople, Egypt, and India too. We Moslems are very much at home wherever the British flag flies. We feel even more secure under the cross of St. George than under the crescent of our Prophet. Why do anything?"

There are more Moslems in India than in Persia and the whole Turkish Empire, including Tripoli, Tunis, Algeria and Morocco, and their Resignation is complete. The Moslem says: "Did not our great Mohammed teach us we should always know whether our caliph had been selected in Heaven or on earth? The caliph who reigns over the largest number of the faithful, whatever his name or title, is the God-chosen caliph." King George reigns over more Mohammedans than all the sultans, khedives and padishahs. May it not be, without changing his religion, George V shall soon be able to call himself, "King of Great Britain, Emperor of India, and Caliph of the Mohammedan world?"

When the Turk recrosses the Bosphorus into Asia, what will he leave behind him in Europe? It is to be hoped he will leave Sancta Sophia — that glorious temple of Christendom—uninjured. He will leave, it is true, a few beautiful palaces which he built in Spain, a large number of exquisite mosques throughout Turkey—but no discoveries, no inventions, no improvements. Constantinople has been greatly improved in the last two years. There are, in some of the streets, excellent pavements, lines of trolleys and electric lights. In a few houses, there are telephones. With these innovations the Turk had nothing to do. Foreign capital, foreign energy and foreign initiative have done it all. The Turk will leave behind him no structures consecrated to science or art, to philanthropy or humanity.

After recrossing the Bosphorus he will mount his horse on the Asiatic side just as his ancestors 500 years ago mounted their horses—horses of the same blood; and there are no better in the world. But his family will follow him in a covered cart, the counterpart of the cart his ancestors used when they came up out of Asia into Europe. The wheels will groan and shriek like the wheels of his forefathers' carts. He will cross lines of railway, some running from Scutari, a short distance into the country, or it may be he will strike the line which is already being built to connect London, Paris and Berlin with Bagdad and Calcutta. But he had nothing to do with any of these lines he would scornfully confess, and he would shed no tears if they were all wiped out.

He will leave behind him in Constantinople a number of schools which were intended primarily for teaching the Will of Allah—as contained in the Koran—nothing else. It is an open question whether even these schools would ever have been established if it had not been that seventy years ago Cyrus Hamlin and men like him came from America to Constantinople. At that time there was no school in the Turkish Empire, and not one school book.

The Turk will leave behind him, up the Bosphorus, a great college in which there are over 600 students. A college to which an American, Mr. Robert, gave $200,000, and to which another American, Mr. John S. Kennedy, gave $1,500,000. In that college many Greeks, Armenians, Bulgarians and some Turks have been educated. The light that has come from that college has been like the discharge of an electric battery upon vegetation which, it is said, so stimulates growth that the fruitage is a hundred-fold what it was before. Greece has felt it, Roumania has felt it, and Bulgaria has been transformed by it.

When the Bulgarians, a little while ago, thought of sending a representative for the first time to the United States they perforce selected a graduate of Robert College, and then, in order that they might be quite sure that they would be adequately and satisfactorily represented, they took not only a graduate but a professor for forty-two years in that college. But the Turk does not love Robert College. He would dynamite it tonight if he could. He does not want anything so disturbing as an educational institution in his philosophy.

Behind him, too, near Robert College, he will leave another and still more offensive centre of western science and learning—a woman's college with 250 students. This is revolutionary and subversive of all his Koran teaches. "Educate a man and you educate an individual. Educate a woman and you educate a family," it has been said. What is to become of the religion of the Prophet when families are educated? The retreating Turk will find forty-four American schools, and 25,000 students in Asia Minor. He will find American colleges at Marsovan, Kharput, Aintab, Tarsus, Marash, and Smyrna. On the Syrian coast at Beyrout he will see another American college with 900 students and thirty-five American teachers and forty native teachers.

As the Turk journeys, wherever he finds a house in which there are either the decencies or the conveniences of civilization, he will know that such a house exists in the Turkish Empire only because either the father or the mother of the family living there was educated in an American or European school.

As he passes through the fields—for there are no roads made by the Turk—he will see his brethren using the agricultural implements of Abraham's time, tickling the soil with a sharp stick as a plow. There are few tools anywhere in the Orient that have not come from the United States. He may cross slopes of mountains in which there are inexhaustible veins of coal and copper, of iron and oil, but if he should travel that country for the next 500 years —the people remaining Moslems—all those resources would be left, as they have been left for the last 700 years, untouched and undeveloped.

When the Turk is once more and forever across the Bosphorus it will be easier to help him than it is now. As an individual he has many attractive qualities. His one virtue, Resignation, has blossomed out into many varieties of beautiful fruit, such as courtesy, geniality, cleanliness, truthfulness, and self-respect, alas, carried to the verge of superciliousness—an extravagant and abnormal sense of his personal superiority. But he has been "cribbed, cabined and confined" in the most constricting creed known to man. He is like a palm—call it a royal palm if you like—planted in a pot. Break the pot—he will be more ready to have it done when he crosses the Bosphorus than he is now—and he may grow to an unrecognizable stature. The hour of his retreat from Europe may thus become the hour of his advance into civilization.

He may be taught then that while Resignation is fundamental, it is only preparatory, like the removing of the stones and roots by which the soil has been encumbered in order that the good seed may be planted. He may be taught then that Evolution, of which he has heard something and which he believes is the European panacea, does not evolve unless it begins with reformation and is carried on by education, and that men and women alike are to receive this education.

The first convert that Mohammed made was his wife, Khadija. Alas that he should have been so ungrateful! He had a place in his paradise for houris but not for women. He teaches, at least by inference, that a woman needs no paradise. Here in our country our women are troubled because they have no vote. In Turkish lands their only trouble is that they have no souls.

Poor Khadija, his first convert, without a soul! A highly educated French woman, a few years or so ago, went to Constantinople and talked to a Turkish woman of high rank about religion, but the Turkish woman said: "Why, I thought religion was a matter only for men." Here in this country there are thousands of men who think that religion is a matter only for women. There is no hope, no possibility of radical reformation for Turkey, so Sir Edwin Pease, who has spent his whole life in Constantinople in most sympathetic contact with the Turk, says, till these two vices upon which Mohammedanism is built— polygamy and slavery—are eradicated. The Moslem women must have schools in which they shall be taught that they have souls, but that the soul withers in polygamy and slavery. When the Turk finds himself in Asia Minor he will be willing, perhaps, to listen to what the twentieth century has to say to him about the advantages of universal education.

He will be ready also to listen when he is told that Resignation is but a half circle, a half hinge; that man must advance from Resignation to Realization if he is to attain to the highest and best possible to him; that "Through love, through hope, through faith's transcendent dower, we feel that we are greater than we know." Only as man has that hope of being something greater than he knows, "only as he apprehends that for which also he is apprehended—the measure of the stature of the fulness of Christ—can he come to "the perfect man." He shall be taught, and he will be ready to listen then, that God is God, but He is the Father of our Lord Jesus Christ, whom even Mohammed called a prophet.

The retreat of Turkey—that hour of her necessity—will be the hour of America's opportunity, not for spoliation, dismemberment or partition, but for redemption and reconstruction. Already we have our representatives in the Turkish Empire. Our "lighthouses," as our schools and colleges have been called, are sending out their rays on that dark and dead coast. Our soldiers are there not to kill and wound, but to give first aid to the wounded. Our cannon are loaded, not with shrapnel, but like most of our cannon along our coasts, with life-lines. It may not be possible even with all our life-saving stations and our lifeboats to keep the waterlogged ship flying the crescent flag from sinking, but surely we shall be able to save thousands of our brothers and sisters who stand calling for help upon the storm-swept decks.

SERBIA, THE BALKANS AND THE WAR

"Knowest thou not that the Philistines are rulers over us?"
Judges 15:11.

When the fabled blast of the bugle startled the sleepers in the enchanted castle, soldiers sprang to arms, and sword clashed against sword, long before the echoes had ceased to reverberate. So a pistol shot in the streets of the little Bosnian town of Serajevo last June aroused all the demons and dogs of war slumbering in Europe. Almost before the echoes had ceased to reverberate, millions of men were in arms. Drawn by an irresistible attraction, like moths to the fire, nine nations are now engaged in a Satanic symphony of war. The madman Herostratus, who flung his torch into the temple of Diana at Ephesus the night Alexander the Great was born, was a harmless lunatic compared with the Serbian student who assassinated the Austrian Archduke and Archduchess. Still, this dastardly deed might have had no more momentous consequences than any other murder of royal personages, had it not been that the whole continent of Europe was so mined that only a shock was needed for the explosion that has split the world.

Europe had long dreaded war as a threatened city dreads the pestilence slowly and visibly creeping toward its walls. Such unintermittent dread produces a condition making the

79

thing dreaded not only a possibility, but a probability. While all these nine nations are fighting fiercely they are each and all indignant if any neutral doubts that they are all fighting a defensive war. All the great powers share the guilt, though they may not be all alike in the measure of their guilt. One and all have been obsessed by the barbaric conviction—shared by many Americans as well as Europeans—that war is the final arbiter of national antagonisms. Theories, it is said, have always more to do with wars than facts. A theory of state rights and slavery caused our Civil War, modern historians assert. The war between Russia and Japan was fought for a theory about zones of influence. This war, the most useless, the most irrational, the most inexcusable that has yet been waged, has been brought about by a theory of economic pressure. That pressure is not yet unendurable in any country, but it may be. Therefore they fight now because they think they may have to fight some day anyhow.

The only logical thing about this war is its source, and that is both logical and psychological.

Political prophets have been saying for years that war was coming. "When war comes it will come from the Balkans." The Balkans produce wars as easily as our Southern States produce cotton, and our States in the great Northwest produce wheat. Germany had a Thirty Years' War, but the Balkans have had wars lasting for three hundred years. The Balkans were at war when Columbus sailed for America, and they were at war, too, when William the Conqueror sailed for England. They have been the inexhaustible fountain, involuntarily, of countless wars.

Once Serbia was supreme in what we call the Balkans— that section of Europe sloping east and west from the mountains of the same name to the Black and Asiatic Seas. In the fourteenth century Serbia controlled Macedonia, Northern Greece, Thessaly and Bulgaria. Her king, Stephen Dushan, had himself crowned Emperor of Greece, Bulgaria and Serbia on Easter Day, in 1346. He released the Greek Church from subservience to the Greek Church of Constantinople. He made his own Archbishop a Patriarch. Doubtless he would have made him Pope, but the Greek Church does not recognize that rank among her clergy. He had his own parliament, as well as his own Patriarch. This parliament passed laws which students tell us compare very favorably with any laws that were passed in the fourteenth century anywhere. He marched on Constantinople for the greatest victory of his life, but on the way he died, when he was only forty-six years old. In thirty-four years from the day of his death the Serbian Empire had ceased to exist.

At the battle of Kossovo the Serbian ruler was captured by the Turk and beheaded. The flower of the Serbian nobility were slaughtered, and the Turk came into complete possession of the Serbian territory. That Serbia was still able to fight after three hundred years of such possession shows what stuff the Serbians are made of. For those three hundred years they would have been compelled to say what the Israelites said in the days of Samson: "Knowest thou not that the Philistine is ruler over us?" You and I thank God that we could never, by any possibility, understand what such servitude must have meant. All their possessions, all their property of every sort, their churches, their families, their honor, were at the mercy of this merciless tyrant.

81

Yet the soul of Serbia did not die. She could still struggle for freedom. She fought a war of eight years, from 1805 to 1813, with the assistance, more or less promissory, of Russia. Then Russia found her own hands full. She was trying to smoke out the great French conqueror from her ancient capital of Moscow. And the Serbian fell once more under the heel of the Turk.

After innumerable vicissitudes, and many changes in dynasties, Serbia came to the promised land of independence in 1882; with a king of her own, not unlike Israel's first King Saul, who fought in vain to break the power of the Philistines. King Milan was like King Saul in his sudden rise to power, in his short-lived popularity, and he was also, unfortunately, like King Saul in his invincible obstinacy. He escaped suicide, the fate of King Saul, by abdication; but left his kingdom very much in the state of Saul's kingdom at his death. King Milan handed over his kingdom to a young successor, who was like the young successor who followed King Saul only in the fact of his extreme youth and his absolute inexperience. King Milan passed on innumerable animosities and scandals that only a David or a Jonathan could have coped with. Young Alexander very soon filled, as might have been expected, the cup of his father's iniquity till he made it overflow by the colossal blunder of his marriage with the unfortunate and unworthy Draga Mashin. Then came the great catastrophe. King Alexander and Queen Draga, abandoned by Russia and Austria, were flung by their so-called friends to the wolves. On the night of June 11, 1903, they made vain efforts to escape. They were found crouching in terror in the palace by a group of Serbian officers, who, it may be, thought themselves patriots of the Brutus type as they plunged their

82

daggers into these pathetic and pleading masses of helplessness that only the day before had worn the crown.

Peter Karageorgevich was chosen to sit on the blood-stained Serbian throne. All that he had to recommend him was the fact that he was the grandson, and that was much of the Prince Kara George, the first leader who had dared lift his hand against the Turk. Whether Peter's hands were stained with the blood of the King and the Queen is an open question—as it is still presumed to be an open question whether Huerta's hands were stained with the blood of Madero.

There came, in 1912, a startling appearance among the nations of Europe. A new nation was suddenly born—less suggestive, it is true, of Minerva, springing fully armed and possessed of more than human wisdom, from the head of Jove—than of Mars, the young god of war, armed with the weapons of the twentieth century. This new nation was called the Balkan Alliance. Wise old statesmen had said: "Such an alliance is a possibility, but it is not a probability." There it was; not a ghost, or specter, but a mysterious and incomprehensible combination of discordant elements. Both friend and foe were amazed. What held these states together it was impossible for anyone to understand who did not know them intimately. But they were so firmly welded that almost from the first every onslaught against the Turk was a victory.

Lulu Burgas followed fast on Kirk Killisseh. Adrianople fell—the first capital and fortress of the Turkish Caliph in Europe. And these conquering armies marched almost to the very walls of Constantinople. The Turk muttered maledictions on the head of the infidel. He tried to stimulate himself with suggestions of victories at Kossovo and a hundred other battlefields.   He recalled the time when these Bulgarians, that were now assaulting his City, were like weeds in his path; when he was free to assassinate as many as he chose while Europe made scarcely a word of protest.   Now the despised vassals were at his throat, clutching his very life!

Twenty-five miles from Constantinople this mysterious army was halted, not by the fortifications alone. These men from Bulgaria, Serbia and Greece, who had so long borne the heavy yoke of Turkey, found their necks strangely chafed by the yoke of this new alliance. The spoils of war were to be divided, and soldiers who had marched shoulder to shoulder, fighting some of the most extraordinary battles of modern times, began to see an abyss yawning at their feet.   Centrifugal forces were separating them.   Under a Satanic spell, so it seems to us, these Allies began to fight with each other more fiercely than they had ever fought against the Turk, who had taught them by long years of oppression to hate him with perfect hatred.

While it is true that in the second Balkan War not everything gained in the first was lost, yet much of the high esteem won from Christendom, by decades of heroism, vanished.

Never again, assuredly, will the Balkans be overrun by Turkish armies.   Never again will assassinations like those ordered by the great assassin, Abdul Hamid, be repeated. Roumania, Bulgaria, Serbia, little Montenegro—that never surrendered to the Turk—Albania, constructively, and Greece are independent sovereignties.   Each has its king and its court.   They are suggestive of the court of the Great Mogul in the treasure house at Dresden.   There are in that toy court 152 figures, all of gold. The throne on which the king sits is gold, the canopy over his head is gold, the slaves who wait by his side are gold, the guards that protect his person are gold, the foundation on which it rests is gold. This court was the product of much time, patience, skill and enormous expense. These sovereignties of the Balkans are also the product of much time, patience, heroism, and a great expenditure of men and money. But, as they stand today, they are like that court of the Grand Mogul in Dresden—just the right size for someone to run off with. Should another Corsican conqueror appear in Europe, what hope will there be for any one of these divided sovereignties of the Balkans? For security and stability they must melt down some of their precious metals over fires seven times heated with the fuel of racial and religious prejudice. Out of this molten mass, when the deadly dross of jealousy and suspicion has been carefully drawn off, may be welded a permanent nation.

There must be an alliance of the Balkans. Pan-Germanism and Pan-Slavism are dreams delightful to some of the emperors and kings of our day; but they are dangerous dreams. They are dreams that will cause the head that wears a crown and welcomes them to lie uneasy. But Pan-Balkanism, like Pan-Americanism, is a dream of quite another sort. They "mean Peace," as Napoleon III said of the Empire—though he knew it was false when he said it.

Young men who see such visions and old men who dream such dreams will never hear the tramp of armed men invading hostile lands or coveted provinces. They will never stain their hands with the blood of those who happen to speak a different language, or to have a different religion, or who chance to have been born and bred under a dif-

85

ferent flag. "Altruistic alliances are academic and visionary," so say the diplomat and the statesman. They exist
in a capital called "Nowhere" of a land named "Bye and
Bye." But a solid wall of partition, that men said could
never be broken down, was broken down for a time in the
Balkans—is broken down tonight in Europe. The Russian
Slav and the Serbian Slav are fighting side by side with
the Irish Celt and the French Celt. The Greek Russian
and the Greek Serbian are fighting side by side with the
Protestant from Great Britain and the Roman Catholic
from Belgium and France. Who dare say that such alliances are impossible because they seem illogical? Who dare
say that such alliances will not endure? Alliances such as
these are destined not only to endure, but to expand, by
intelligence, by civilization, by common sense, till all men
shall stand on the same table land where women stand today,
hating the monster of war, within whose Moloch-like jaws
they have seen millions of their sons disappear forever.

Who dare say that we may not have the "United States
of Europe," "A parliament of man, a federation of the
world?" Pray for it, look for it. "Though it tarry, wait
for it—it will surely come, it will not tarry."

Possibly we may find extreme difficulty in taking as
much interest religiously in Serbia with its established
Church—a Church in which the Serbians themselves say
there have been incorporated many ceremonies and rites
of Paganism—as we take in Bohemia, Hungary and Austria, lands that were for a time under the sway of the
ideals of civil and religious liberty which make up so large
a part of our Protestantism. It is true now even in those
lands that these ideas are like the disappearing rivers, of
which some travellers tell us, that suddenly vanish only to

rise further on with increased volume of fertilizing waters expanding over an ever enlarging area. May such be the future of the vanished river of reformed religion in Bohemia, Hungary and Austria!

But Serbia! We should not be fair to Serbia, we should not be just to ourselves, should we forget tonight a twelfth century movement in Serbia for simplicity, sincerity, purity, in religion. There came out of Bulgaria a priest named Bogoomil, who taught in Serbia with large acceptance before Luther had spoken in Wittenberg, Huss in Prague, or Wycliff in Oxford.

Bogoomil, like Erasmus, saw bishops, priests and monks living idle, luxurious and even immoral lives. He saw, like Mohammed, among the corrupt Christians with whom he associated, multitudes of people worshipping images of the Madonna and the saints, and relying on relics, as if in them the great God, Himself, was imprisoned.

He thought, like John Knox, that the Bible is the only infallible rule of faith and practice; and, like George Fox, and many of the Protestants of our own day, that no Christian needs any intermediary, either prelate or saint, between his soul and God. He believed, like Tolstoy, that there may be helpful religious services without any priest or minister being present, and that all prayers and services should be in the tongue of the people. Like Tolstoy he taught the supremacy of benevolence and love, and that war, all war, is an offense to the God and Father of our Lord Jesus Christ.

This was in the twelfth century. The Serbians were sympathetic toward such teaching. Groups of them were formed who called themselves: "Bogoomil, the dear children of God." They were in some respects not unlike our Quakers, who call themselves: "Friends of God." They were noted not only for their simplicity, and sincerity, but for their truthfulness and honesty. But they were schismatics, The established Church and the hierarchy with the sovereign and the aristocracy looked upon them with more than disfavor—with extreme disapprobation. They tried to exterminate them. It took three hundred years to do it. What was left of the movement was almost entirely eradicated by Moslem misrule that swept over the Balkans like a forest fire leaving in great sections scarcely a trace even of Christianity. The majority of the Bosnian nobles, it is said, became Moslems. The Serbian priests thought of themselves not so much as pastors or preachers, as patriots —which they were. It seemed to them a more important thing to fight against the Turk than against "the world, the flesh and the devil."

One of the most highly educated and intelligent of the modern Serbian priests said to a Scotchman, who was urging upon him the importance of more prayer among the people—"We have relied too much on prayer; what we want is not prayer, but schools, soldiers, and, most of all, guns." If we had lived where that Serbian priest lived, if we had been surrounded, even as our forefathers were for a little while surrounded by Indians—if we had been in subjection for three hundred years to the Sioux—and the Sioux were never more cruel than the Turk—it might very easily have come to pass that the comparative value of schools, soldiers, guns, and prayer would have been somewhat confused in our minds.

The sun of the twelfth century, pro-Protestantism in Serbia, may have sunk to rise no more, but there is a new dawn in the East. The brightest rays of it are falling upon Bulgaria, but the light is spreading over all the Balkans. It is the light that breaks from the English and the American schools in the Turkish Empire. In those schools men from all parts of the Balkans are taught that across the sea there is a nation of 80,000,000 of men and women, the richest nation—and let us speak it modestly—we hope the most benevolent and generous nation on the face of the earth; the nation that has given to Turkey the larger number of these schools. In these United States of America the people are sovereigns. They govern themselves. In the capital of this nation there are no royal palaces, but there is not a village in all the land where there is not a school, and very few villages in which there are not churches; while this nation has a small, almost invisible army and a little navy, it has no forts and no warships along 4,000 miles of its frontier, where flies a foreign flag side by side with the Stars and Stripes. In these schools they will learn that peace between these two strong, dominant, ambitious nations has been preserved for a hundred years, not by soldiers, and not by guns, but by prayer and Christian principles.

AUSTRIA-HUNGARY AND THE WAR

"If, therefore, the Son shall make ye free, ye shall be free indeed." John 8:36.

The roots of Austria's most glorious successes and most ignominious defeats, of her strength and of her weakness are deeply imbedded in the dark shadows and cavernous depths of the indescribable and inchoate Holy Roman Empire. For ten centuries—from the year 800 to 1806—this empire held sway over the larger part of Europe by sword and by imagination. When Charlemagne had himself crowned on Christmas Day in the year 800 at St. Peter's in Rome, he was called the "Emperor of the West," so reviving, as he believed, the old Empire of Rome, of which he thought himself the inheritor. But the term "Holy Roman Empire" was not used until the time of Barbarossa, in the twelfth century.

The mighty "Red-beard," with his haughty manner and his imperial plans, was nevertheless so beloved and honored that legends of him in song and story are still told in Germany and in Italy. This Roman sceptre, supposed to carry with it imperial authority over Europe, passed from hand to hand, till it came to the Hapsburgs, who held it for something over 400 years. The Emperor was elected, according to the Golden Bull of 1356, by seven electors—the term Elector means much still in Europe—one king, the King of Bohemia; three archbishops, of Mainz, Treves and Cologne;

one duke, the Duke of Saxony; one margrave, the Margrave of Brandenburg, and one count, the Count Palatine of the Rhine.

These seven Electors registered votes which they supposed recorded the will of Heaven. The Emperor so elected, and with such tremendous power, naturally took himself very seriously. He was a unique personage. "Only Emperors are great," said a king, who had tried to be elected Emperor and had failed: "Only Emperors are great." And the Emperor thought so too. He had to play the part. He had to be every inch of him Emperor of the Holy Roman Empire. He found himself not only seated on an imperial throne, but encircled by laws and customs and edicts, some of which unlike those "fine customs that curtsy to great kings" were unyielding.

The Emperor wore the robe of Cæsar, and he must have the stride of an Augustus. He was necessarily champion of the Church whose hands had rested in benediction on his head. He was compelled to hate all heretics and unsheath his sword against all schismatics. The Holy Roman Empire began in an assumption—the assumption of Charlemagne, and ended in an abdication—the abdication of Francis I of Austria.

So long as the Empire was in the hands of the Hapsburgs it was easy for Austria to make her voice heard in the councils of Europe. But the voice of the people was not heard in her courts and their interests were not considered in the deliberations of her rulers. Austria since the days of the Hapsburgs has always been the logically consistent antagonist of democracy—of the rule of the people—and she has been the persistent and unintermittent champion and advocate of authority, autocracy and the supremacy of the Church. She has always been a strong-hold in the time of trouble for mediævalism.

It is an unfortunate thing for Austria—or for us—that most of us received our first impressions of Austria, and the Austrian way of doing things, from our school histories, in reading the story of our boyhood's hero, Richard the Lion-Heart, and his imprisonment by Duke Leopold of Austria. Richard was always ready by night or by day to call for his charger, jump into his armour, seize his sword, and fight the pagan, Salladin, with part or all his army. Richard, returning from Palestine, passing with the Crusader's pledge of safety through Austria, was betrayed near Vienna. Imprisoned in a high tower, he thought himself forgotten by the whole world, until the day Blondel, his court musician, sang one of the old songs beneath his window, to which Richard responded. When Leopold found it impossible to hold this famous prisoner longer, he demanded an enormous ransom from him, which, it is said, impoverished Richard to his dying day. When we compared Salladin and his pagan courtesy and chivalry, with this Austrian Duke and his cupidity, we always felt that the pagan was the true knight "without fear and without reproach."

Bohemia was not a part of Austria when John Huss was born. Not until a hundred years later was it incorporated with Austria. Yet the Emperor of the Holy Roman Empire of that day was, of course, as powerful at Constance as at Budapest, and therefore the burning of John Huss, like the imprisonment of Richard "yea and nay" lies at Austria's door. Huss was the lineal, spiritual descendant of John Wycliff, of England. When Huss boldly preached in the University of Prague, of which he was the rector, doctrines like those of Wycliff; when he announced

93

to that highly educated, academic world, that "the authority of the Scriptures is superior to the authority of the Pope and of councils; that in matters concerning salvation, God alone may have rule over the consciences of men"—it became impossible for him to live in the Holy Roman Empire.

Huss went to Constance under the safe conduct of Sigismund, the Emperor. There he was tried before a council and condemned to the stake. On the 6th of July, 1415, they took this "pale, thin man, in mean raiment," as the chronicler describes him, and unfrocked him, metaphorically. They hacked the spurs from his heels. They broke his sword. They led him out under the blue sky to a great tree a little way from the blue lake, and tied him to the stake, and lighted the pile—it may be with that very scrap of paper on which Sigismund had written his "safe conduct." When only ashes were left, they gathered them together and flung them into the Rhine, that the whole world might see what the Holy Roman Empire does to the man who dares permit his soul to grow holy in any other way than by the permit of Holy Church.

Just a hundred years after John Huss, the German monk Luther was summoned before the Diet of Worms, by the Hapsburg Emperor Charles V, the greatest Emperor of modern times, to answer for his revolt against authority and his treatment of the Papal Bull. Thomas Carlyle calls this "The greatest scene in modern European history." The "little monk" stood alone while the representative of the Emperor, and the representative of the Pope, and all the high dignitaries of the Church and the Empire scowled at him. With his feet firmly planted on the rock of responsibility to God, and not to man, he cries: "Here I stand! I cannot do otherwise; God help me." God did help him. The "safe conduct" would have been as worthless for him as it was for John Huss. But his friends waylaid him and carried him in triumph to the secure seclusion of the Wartburg.

In a hundred years more this rank heresy that had been taught by Wycliff and Huss and Luther had spread through Germany, into Bohemia and Hungary and even into Austria itself. The Emperor saw that both the Holy Roman Empire and the Holy Roman Church were alike threatened. Every effort was exerted to extinguish the flame lighted by fire that had fallen from Heaven.

In 1620 the Emperor sent his ultimatum to the Protestants at Prague. These Protestants—we are not always consistent, we Protestants—made a very un-Protestant protest to the impossible demand of the Emperor. They took his representatives by the heels and flung them out of the window. That was the beginning of the Thirty Years' War, in which more than twenty million persons perished. All the decisive defeats that Protestantism received during those entire thirty years were at the hands of the representatives of the Holy Roman Empire, and by the Bohemian General, Wallenstein.

But of all the strange exhibitions that Austria or any other land has ever seen of the antagonism of the reactionary element to the modern progressive spirit, the strangest was that in the days of Joseph II. He was the son of Maria Theresa, whose sex was so lost in her sovereignty that when she appeared before her courtiers in Hungary, they cried: "We will die for our *King* Maria Theresa."

Joseph did not have her soul. He had the soul of a Washington. If he and Washington could have changed places, they might have changed fates. He was an autocrat by birth. He was the Emperor of Austria-Hungary and of the Holy Roman Empire. But he was a democrat. He was ready to resist autocracy by every instrument in his power.

He refused to be crowned because his coronation oath compelled him to exercise distasteful authority. He divided his Empire into thirteen provinces, each of which had all the Home Rule Ireland is demanding for herself today. He withstood the Church of Rome and commanded his Bishops and Cardinals not to give obedience to the Pope when his commands were in opposition to Austrian edicts. He dissolved 900 monasteries and convents and told the monks and the nuns to go to work for God and man and earn an honest living.

He took the schools out of the hands of the ecclesiastics, who had no respect for liberty of conscience in child or parent, and gave them over to the State pledged to toleration. "But the light shined in the darkness and the darkness comprehended it not." Everywhere in Austria, everywhere throughout the Holy Roman Empire, Joseph was antagonized. When he was obeyed, it was sullenly and scoffingly; often he was derided and defied. He died, at last, as Washington probably would have died under the same circumstances, of a broken heart. Austria did her best to bury him so deep that humanity might forget him forever under a single word, "Josephinism," intended to be more completely and contemptuously obliterating than oblivion itself. No Emperor of Austria, no Emperor of the Holy Roman Empire ever tried again to play the role of Reformer.

Francis I, the father-in-law of Napoleon Bonaparte, and one of those who assisted in giving the quietus to the great

French Emperor, concluded that the time had come, in 1806, when he could no longer afford to play the role that Hobbes had described as the "Ghost of the Empire sitting crowned upon the Empire's grave." There was not enough left of the Empire for a military funeral. Francis abdicated the imperial throne as gladly as Charlmagne, a thousand years before, assumed it.

Francis presided over the Holy Alliance, which met in 1815 in Vienna, and proved to the satisfaction of everyone that, though he had changed his title, he had not changed his character.

He was still as reactionary as the noblest Roman Emperor of them all. He was more than pleased when he was chosen to turn back the hand on the dial to the place where it stood in the days of the Bourbons. Everything that his imperial son-in-law had done for himself, and incidentally for France; everything that had been accomplished by the Revolution in its violence, and by Napoleon in his ambition—all by-products which might have been valuable to humanity—were swept away by that Holy Alliance. How many crimes have been committed in the name "Holy," as in that other name "Liberty!"

The last of the liberators to be crushed by the hand of Austria was Kossuth—though it must be acknowledged Austria did her very best to put Garibaldi on the same roll of honor.

In 1848 a wave of revolt against autocracy swept over all Europe. It seemed at one time that it would engulf Berlin, Paris and Vienna. Out of that tumult came a hero-patriot, Kossuth. At last Hungary had a hero of her own. Better than that, she had a patriot. A patriot is something in all lands and in all times, nobler than a hero. Kossuth gathered around him a little mob-like army, which was defeated. But the cause of liberty was not defeated, and liberty, though she must wait will yet be crowned both in Budapest and in Vienna.

Kossuth was compelled, like a great many men of his time, in Germany as well as in Austria-Hungary, after the revolutionary year of 1848, to flee the country.

Many of these patriots came to America and speedily took their places among our most useful citizens. Never has a foreigner since Lafayette been greeted with such enthusiasm, it is said, as that with which Kossuth was welcomed. Austria could not understand it. Here was one of her outlaws feted like a conqueror. Austria is not alone in finding great difficulty in understanding the American point of view. All Europe labors under that difficulty. It is for the European quite incredible that there should be for America no interests imaginable greater than liberty, democracy—the right of the people to choose their own rulers and to say how they shall be ruled.

There never ought to be a moment's doubt as to where America is to stand on any such issue. The instant we know that our would-be friends have lined themselves up against freedom of conscience in religion and in the State, that instant we know they have lined themselves up against us and we against them.

It may be true that in this terrible war which now threatens to dismember Austria, leaving her either the vassal of Germany or the victim of the Allies—a war which threatens to disrupt European civilization and wreck Europe itself—we have formed our judgment

98

on what may appear to be, years hence, when accurate history is written, inadequate grounds. But the world must know that our judgments are always formed on what we think are the principles for which our fathers fought, and for which they gave up their country, and came to these shores, making here their great venture for humanity.

The needle in the American compass may seem to sweep suddenly around a semi-circle. The scales may appear to rise or fall with amazing rapidity, but the needle is always true to the pole of principle, and the scales go up and down according to the weight of what we take for evidence.

In the last ten years more immigrants have come to the United States from Austria-Hungary than from any other part of the world. We call them Slovacs. There is nothing about them to suggest our Puritan forefathers. They are not even, for the most part, disciples of John Huss. They are largely members of the Greek or the Roman Catholic Churches—or they are unchurched altogether. They are not highly educated, they have very little *gemuthlickeit* for which the Austrians are famous, and almost none of their culture. Many of them are illiterate and ignorant. They have never even heard the names, it may be, of Beethoven, Handel and Schubert—but they are humanity in the rough. They are "the stuff out of which nations may be carved." They are strong and industrious, and they are needed in our fields and factories. They are responsive, wonderfully responsive, to the American environment. They need only a few months here, most of them, before learning to remove their hats when the

"Star Spangled Banner" is played or sung, and they have learned, at the same time, not to kneel when the proprietor of the little tenement, or shack, in which they live, passes by. Their artistc taste becomes quickly so refined that they are sure that the statue of Liberty in New York harbor is the finest statue in the world!

Their children, or their children's children, coming up through our public schools, will not only know more than their fathers and their grandfathers, and have better manners and houses than they, but they will be better educated, better mannered and better housed than some of the children of parents who now look upon these Slovacs as barbarians.

When they have spent a year or two in this country, and return home for a visit, they ship in the steerage which some one has said is the "first cabin, twice removed." But they are first class emissaries of decency and comfort, of Liberty, Equality and Fraternity. When they have stayed a few more years in this country, they will go back as veritable missionaries; missionaries of civilization, and some of them, at least, of a reformed and rational Christianity.

They will replant—these children of the Slovac, educated here in America—in that soil which has been torn and rent by war, and stained by the blood of soldiers and patriots and martyrs, the seed planted long ago by John Huss and Martin Luther, Joseph II and Kossuth. From that seed, in the twentieth century, will come harvests greater and more glorious than those for which the reformers and patriots toiled and fought and prayed.

HOLLAND AND THE WAR

"A little one shall become a thousand, and a small one a strong nation."   Isaiah 60:22.

"The inverted bowl we call the sky," of which Omar Khayyam sings, fits so perfectly on the bowl, right side up, we call Holland, that the foreigner feels in Holland like a colossal fly imprisoned between two saucers. Looking up from a level thirty to sixty feet below the sea, the rim of the bowl cuts the sharp skyline beneath which the waves roar as if eager to devour either the lid or the body of the bowl.

The history of this shut-in land has been, in academic language, a prolonged and unintermittent "bowl fight." Which side was to get the bowl and keep it? That was the question. Was it to belong to the farmer or to the sailor, to the cows or to the fishes, to the Netherlanders or to Neptune? This long, ceaseless struggle has not exhausted but stimulated the Hollander. The salt of the sea has kept his courage fresh and his spirit strong. The Dutch farmer is as bluff, hearty and vigorous as the Dutch sailor.

But this struggle has settled forever the physical aspects of the country. In these low, fat fields, fat cattle, owned by fat men, milked by fair, if not fat, maidens, will always feed.

From these fields brooms have swept back the sea as Xerxes in vain commanded his soldiers to do; but the Dutch have used the broom more scientifically than the Persian autocrat. They have planted broom corn on the dykes in such a way that it binds the soil in a living network from which structure the seductive waves cannot tear it. Dotting these fields are numberless windmills, whose long, flapping arms are frightful enough in the twilight to keep a Don Quixote perpetually in the saddle, with lance in rest ready to ride down upon these monsters, evidently bent on devouring the fat cattle and the fair maidens.

Here and there, in the corners of these fields, myriads of tulips, with colors more exquisitely gorgeous than any oriental carpet, push their heads through the rich soil like fairies delivered by the sun god from the dark prisons of dusky slave dealers. Here peasants toil with all the zest with which the tillers of the fields in other lands make soberly merry on feast days and church festivals. Here the fisher-folk, in some towns, at least, wear curious garments, richly ornamented, as if expecting, momentarily, to join the other guests at a wedding which never takes place.

"This land beyond the sea" is the antithesis of the Amalfi, of which Longfellow loved to dream, but it, too, has a charm which has inspired poets and painters. It has a history as splendid and heroic as Amalfi's. "A little one, here, has become a thousand, and a small one a strong nation." Only 150 miles long and 120 broad, Holland has a population of but six millions, yet its colonies number thirty-eight millions posessing 730,000 square miles, in Java, Sumatra and Borneo, of the East Indies.

Holland's struggle with the sea, in which this gigantic bowl of milk and cheese and tulips was the prize.

with the possession of a highly profitable trade thrown in, was a stimulating sport compared with her struggle with Spain for "a place in the sun," with liberty to move around in that place, for work or for worship, as she might choose.

In the Sixteenth Century Holland was the Italy of Northern Europe, not only because some of her canalized cities like Amsterdam were suggestive of Venice, but because of her *naisance,* her birth—it was not a *renaissance,* as in Italy—in science, art and commerce.

Falling, by unfortunate marriages for her, into the merciless hands of the Holy Roman Emperors, Holland found herself at last in the clutches of Charles V, the Hapsburg autocrat. He was the most powerful man in the world at that time. He was the antagonist of Luther, and of liberty in every form in both church and state. Inheriting the Netherlands, he rubbed his hands with the cruel delight the sea must have felt when it swept away the dikes, and saw many fair gardens at its mercy.

Charles was religiously a multi-millionaire, but morally he was a pauper. He had religion, such as it was, to give away to those who were already satisfied with the one they had, and who respectfully declined that which he attempted to force on them with devices in which the Spanish Inquisition was expert. He pacified Ghent as Louvain and Termonde were pacified a few months ago, but showing more foresight he impoverished without destroying, having in mind the possibility of many profitable repetitions.

103

His son, Philip, lacked his father's courage and power to compel fear if not respect, but Philip's bigotry was a much more real thing than his father's. Philip was less hypocritical than Charles, though not less immoral, but his consistency was unquestioned. He hated all schismatics with a holy hatred so complete that it made no exceptions for Protestant generals who might have been extraordinarily useful to him in certain exigencies.

Philip's chosen emissary in Holland was the Duke of Alva. He was, spiritually and Satanically, bone of Philip's bone and flesh of his flesh. Between Alva and the sea, the Hollanders never hesitated when the choice was left to them—that may have been the origin of the adage: "Between the devil and the deep sea."—The sea was cruel, but with no such refinement of inconceivable cruelty as Alva.

In the coils of this dragon Holland was the damsel about to be crushed, and the St. George to give his life-blood to deliver her was William of Orange, as noble a knight as ever rode to the rescue of distressed womanhood. William was either unknown to Lord Byron or forgotten by him, or, it may be the noble Lord could not think of a good rhyme for William, or he never would have made our Washington the one and only name in all the list of the world's worthies, unstained by "guilty glory" or "despicable state."

Motley may have painted William, as Cromwell's court painter wished to paint the Protector, "without wart or wrinkle, or any such thing." But after all necessary or possible deductions, Motley's hero stands in the center of that bowl, against which the sea and

104

Spaniard raged, one of the most splendid specimens of humanity in the world's history.

William fell like Moses on the borders of the Land of Promise. Philip, who laughed out loud when he was told about St. Bartholomew's Day, must at least have smiled with devout satisfaction when he heard that his hired assassin had earned the gold for which he had sold himself to Satan.

Three other shining names are written high on Holland's roll of fame: John Van Barneveldt, the victim of religious bigotry, called Protestant, which was only a little less repulsive than the bigotry of Philip, himself; John DeWitt, the victim of political bigotry, which may be as deadly but is not so virulent as the religious form; William III, great-grandson of William the Silent, the husband of Mary, daughter of James II of England. Related to Great Britain by marriage as Charles and Philip were to Holland, William might have proved as great an incubus to his relations-in-law as the Spanish kings were to theirs. But to Macaulay and to all lovers of popular rights William's coming to England was like his great-grandfather's coming to Holland from the German city of his birth—a benediction.

England was then eagerly scanning the horizon for a knight of the right kind, and at first no one thought he might be hidden by the rim of that "Bowl." The same dragon that had so nearly crushed Holland held England in his coils. Religious liberty and every other kind of liberty was gasping. Then came William and Mary and James—a pale reproduction of Philip—slunk away with his Romish retinue to the safe shores of France.

That Great Britain, since the revolution of 1688, has marched at the head of the army of progress, is in no small degree due to William and Mary, who broke the shackles from the souls of men and turned slaves to soldiers.

America's debt to Holland, while not so vast as that of Great Britain, is at least so large that we gratefully confess we never expect to pay it. The Dutch colonists coming to our shores in 1614, were of less heroic stature mentally and spiritually, if not physically, than the Pilgrims who arrived at Plymouth in 1620, or the Puritans who came to New England ten years later. The Dutch colonists were looking for liberty, not to worship, but to barter.

Holland had sent Henry Hudson, the English sailor, in 1609, to find a northwest passage to India. That supposed passage, like the supposed Elixir of Life and the Fountain of Youth and the Philosopher's Stone "led countless generations on," many to death, and a few like Hudson to glory. Five years after Hudson sailed up the river a fort was built at Albany. Nine years later a trading station was established on Manhattan, called New Amsterdam. It consisted of a flagstaff, a tall warehouse, a church, and a dozen or so one-storied houses with Dutch roofs.

Captured by the English in 1664—the English thought it most incongruous for these foreigners to cut in between their colonies in New England and New Jersey—the name was changed to New York. But the Dutch flavor, like the scent of the roses in the broken vase, "hung round it still." Dutch names are stamped, not only on the river itself, but on many of the streets of the two cities at either end, and on the villages between. Dutch customs, Dutch stability and steadfastness, sometimes to the verge of stolidity, have been inwrought into the character of the people.

The Dutch Reformed Church preserved all that was best in the mother church, and added the fire of missionary zeal. It is one of our aggresive Protestant churches. It has no intention of repeating the mistake the Dutch made in some colonies, where they built great churches but no schools, and compelled the natives to attend the services, as Francis Xavier compelled the natives of India to be baptized, and both Protestant and Roman Catholic, alike, reverted, when the restraint was removed, to their original Paganism. This American Dutch church has adopted modern methods with lines of circumvallation for slow but sure approach to the forts and fortresses of the enemy. They have built churches, chapels, schools, academies and hospitals for the conquest of ignorance, superstitution and sin.

This reformed and Americanized church has carried the war even into the heart of Asiatic Mohammedanism. Within a few days' march of Mecca, on the shores of the Red Sea, where Mohammed drove his camels, the sappers and miners of this salvation army are at work. These inheritors of the traditions, if not the fortunes, of the Dutch colonists are in that land of terrible desert and unendurable heat, because they were inspired by the heroism of a young Englishman, who gave his life to the seemingly forlorn hope of an Arabic mission.

The youngest son of Lord Kintore, an elder in the Scotch Free Church, the Honorable Ion Keith Falconer, was a giant physically and a prizewinner in intercollegiate, athletic, and intellectual contests. A brilliant career was open to him, both politically, diplomatically, and academically. To such qualities as his, combined with such influence as he could exert, everything is possible in Great Britain.

Hearing a call that rang as loud and clear in his soul as the call that made Saul of Tarsus a missionary to the Gentiles, young Falconer went to Arabia and there, after two years' service, he died, the glorious death of a martyr, for Christ's sake. "Of all pulpits," says John Ruskin, "from which the human voice is ever sent forth, there is none from which it reaches so far as from the grave." Falconer's voice, heard only in subdued tones in the lecture halls of Cambridge, now carried from the grave across the sea, and the young Americans of the Reformed Church heard his challenge, took up his sword, and are today fighting the battle from which he was summoned to his coronation.

It is not defeat, wounds and death that appall; it is meaninglessness—the paralyzing conviction that the game is not worth the candle. Self-sacrifice for a great and glorious cause is never useless, never too costly, is never regretted by those who make it or by those who understand it. The sword that cuts the nerve of faith and hope is the sword swung in the hand of hate or ambition, of pride or envy; the sword whose swish sounds in the ears of five or six million soldiers in Europe tonight.

To die fighting, as Falconer died, to make men free, to break down prison doors, to open all God's world to God's children, to educate the ignorant, to care for the sick and wounded in hospitals more comfortable than any oriental palace, to tell the dying of an eternal life of endless growth and blessedness, is to make death so glorious that the splendor of it illumines life's most commonplace details. But to die as fearless men are dying today in the trenches

of France and Poland, and in the passes of the Carpa-
thians, who do not know why or for what they are dying,
is a holocaust of horror over which coming generations
will wring their hands in shame and pity.

Little Holland peaceful and contended, asking only to be
let alone, cultivating with plodding Dutch assiduity, all
those arts of peace, which produce the plenty and prosperity,
in which all the world must share, is a high Rembrandt
light, increasing the intense density of the shadow that
darkens the rest of Europe where the great powers are
struggling to become greater by destruction and slaughter.

Twice the nations have heard a call to a Peace Conference in Holland's modest "House in the Woods," at The
Hague. The Palace of Peace which American generosity built not far away for future conferences is desolate
and silent, but a lute-like note sounds from the cities,
towns and villages of Holland like the subdued music
of the Bells of Is, calling Emperors and Kings to stop
the mad and murderous onslaught of soldiers, and imitate Holland in her "more excellent way," and no longer
cast covetous eyes on the vineyards of any Naboth.

"A little one shall become a thousand, and a small
one a strong nation," not by conquest, spoliation and
robbery, but by righteousness, fair dealing and a patriotism so broad as to include all nations made by God
of one blood.

ITALY AND THE WAR

'And he said unto them, The kings of the Gentiles exercise lordship over them; and they that exercise authority upon them are called benefactors. But ye shall not be so." Luke 22:25 and 26.

As we speak the name Italy a canvas unrolls itself as vast as the frescoes of the Sistine Chapel, where Michael Angelo massed gigantic figures telling the story of the progress of humanity from the moment of creation. On this canvas is painted "the most spectacular history in human annals"—the history of Italy. Here is depicted the origin and development of our modern world. Our culture, language and laws came from Greece, through Rome, where an indelible impress was made upon them, which is clearly distinguishable underneath the later inscriptions made in France, England and Germany.

When the Roman Empire, which had held the world for centuries in its sway, was at last overwhelmed by the barbarians who swept down like a cyclone from the north, the destruction was so complete that fourteen centuries passed before the work of restoration was carried to the point where it was possible to speak of a *Renaissance*—a new birth.

Even then this new birth was partial and incomplete. Italy, it is true, was reborn artistically and intellectually in the Fifteenth and Sixteenth Centuries, but nationally she was still "powerless to be born." Metternich, the Austrian diplomat, could speak of her sneeringly but accurately as late as the Nineteenth Century, as a "geographical expression." To diplomats of Metternich's day and school it was flatly unbelievable that Italy should ever be anything else. Sentimentally she was, as Browning calls her:

> "The woman-country, wooed, not wed;
> Loved all the more by earth's male lands."

No country is comparable to her in charm—there is no other country whose æsthetic, artistic and literary courtship has been so long and ardent.

As a geographical and poetical expression Italy had a place of her own in all hearts if not on the maps and in the books, and "in the sun." Hers was an incomparable inheritance historically, archæologically and æsthetically, but it was an impossible and irresistible inheritance after all of bad blood infected with virulent Cæsarism and imperialism in both State and Church. Disunited, dismembered, broken up into many principalities and dukedoms, and one ecclesiastical domain, each of the political parts was complete only as a maw and a stomach eager to devour and digest all the other parts.

The ecclesiastical domain was the hungriest of all, with an abnormal appetite which nothing but the whole of Italy and Europe could have satisfied, even temporarily. The white-robed Vicar of Christ in the Vatican could never forget the day when a Hildebrand could order Emperors to act as stable boys and hold his stirrups while he climbed into the saddle. With such memories every pope found it hard to recall that other day when his Master took the servant's place and announced as a finality: "The kings of the Gentiles exercise lordship over them, and they that exercise authority upon them are called benefactors. But ye shall not be so." "Among you he is greatest and most Godlike who serves most and best."

The heart of Italy, the Vatican, before the Nineteenth Century, was suffering from fatty degeneration, the degeneration that comes from pride, self-seeking, and secularism. Italy's blood was blue, but thickened with pernicious substances, and only slowly forced by abnormally high pressure into the extremities twisted with gout and rheumatism and trembling with inefficiency and feebleness. In whatever direction Italy lifted her eyes "filled with tears of distress, and her white brow on which sorrow was ploughed by shame," as Byron wrote, she saw either avowed enemies or unreliable friends.

Austria openly acknowledged that she counted on being Italy's residuary legatee on her final demise, and she had no hesitation is saying Italy was "an unconscionable time in dying." If a few well-directed efforts on Austria's part could shorten Italy's suffering they would be immediately forthcoming.

France modulated her voice till this "woman country" had reason to fear that she was not only being wooed but might be forcibly wed by her somewhat too ardent northern lover. That proved, indeed, to be her fate.

When Napoleon, in 1805, was crowned King of Italy at Milan, with the iron crown of Monza, and his brother,

Joseph, in 1806, was enthroned at Naples by a similar, though less gorgeous ceremony, and the Pope, Pius VII, was brought a virtual prisoner to Fontainebleau in 1809, the fate of Italy seemed no longer in doubt.

But there were living forces still in Italy. Undreamed of possibilities were before her. Napoleon's grip was at last broken. When he sailed away a prisoner to St. Helena all the Bonaparte kinglets dropped their crowns and scurried for some place of safety. "A cry of pain" from all parts of Italy stirred a patriotism that was not dead but soundly sleeping. Young men like Mazzini, Cavour and Garibaldi saw visions of an Italian *Renaissance,* when Italy should be reborn not alone artistically and intellectually, as in the days of Florentine splendor under the Medicean lovers of luxury and beauty, but haters of liberty and unity.

Cavour, Count of Piedmont, then called Sardinia, saw more distinctly than either Mazzini or Garibaldi the possibility and necessity of a "coalition not of princes but of the people." With a fiery zeal like that of Peter the Hermit calling Europe to a crusade against pagans whose defiling hands held sacred places, Cavour with much greater intelligence, if not eloquence, called all Italians to rise against the tyrants, whose contaminated hands had crushed the liberties of the people. He used the pen, but Garibaldi used the sword and wore a red shirt and though Garibaldi did far less for Italy than Cavour, the man of the pen is unknown to many foreigners to whom the man of the sword is a popular hero. Whoever bathes the conqueror's sword in blood and wears a notable costume will have an immediate popularity denied to the patriot who relies on the pen or the voice

114

to awaken sleeping humanity. But in redeemed and liberated Italy Cavour is as much greater than Garibaldi as, in America, Lincoln is greater than Grant.

Cavour did not live to see the day—it could never have dawned had he not lived and labored for it—that September day in 1870, when the Italian cannon battered down the walls of Rome and Italian troops marched in through the Porta Pia, and Italy ceased to be "a geographical expression." Italy was placed once more on the map with its own Italian king, Victor Emmanuel, who, though by no means a Washington, was a true father of his country, deserving a better fate than to be elevated at the end of the Roman Corso in an inartistic apotheosis, by the most grandiose monument in Europe.

Rome is at the same time the most ancient and the most modern of capitals. The city of Romulus and Remus, of Cæsar and Cicero, of Peter and Paul, is the city that became once more the Italian capital, after centuries of foreign and prelatical domination, when Victor Emmanuel entered in triumph in July, 1872.

As Rome is the newest comer among capitals, so Italy is the latest arrival among the great powers. Only in 1882 was she admitted as an equal to their councils. Now she finds herself wooed with impetuous ardour by Kaisers and Kings, by Czar and President, each and all of her wooers, like Penelope's suitors, indignantly refusing to take "No" for an answer. Were it not for her well-equipped navy and army the world might see the "Rape of the Sabine Women" repeated, with Italy in the title role. Fortunately there is no danger that the

day will return of which Byron sang of Italy almost in
the words of an early Italian sonnet:

"Oh, God! that thou wert in thy nakedness
 Less lovely or more powerful, and couldest claim
 Thy right and awe the robbers' band who press,
 To shed thy blood and drink the tears of thy distress."

Italy responded more wholeheartedly than any other
land, as was to have been expected, in the greatest intellectual and artistic revival Europe has yet seen—
the Renaissance.   This widespread beneficent movement was, as Amiel, the philosopher of Geneva, saw
clearly, impartial and incomplete.   In speaking of one
whose "horizon is that of the Renaissance," Amiel says:
"The religious note is absent from its lyre.   There is
nothing in him which shows any contact with Christianity, any knowledge of the sublime tragedies of the soul.
Kind nature is his goddess, Horace his prophet, and
Montaigne his gospel.   This division of things is common in Italy, too.   It is the natural effect of political
religion.   The priest becomes separated from the lay-
man, the believer from the man, worship from sincerity."

Italy has never been without a saving remnant who
have not bowed the knee to the Baal of absolutism,
clericalism, and prelatical infallibility, in itself the negation of the existence of God and his ever-present ac-
tivity.

When King Humbert, some years ago, received dele-
gations from the various religious organizations of Italy
he looked bewildered.   Some were introduced by names,

whose denominations were evidently altogether unknown to him, but when the Waldensian ministers approached, the king said with a smile which included approval as well as recognition: "Ah, I know you Waldenses." And well he might! Some of his ancestors had known them not too wisely if too well. They were inspired, these dukes of Savoy, by the same misapprehension of Christian principles and permanent forces that had annihilated the Albigenses—the predecessors of the Waldensians—"A war distinguished even among the wars of religion by merciless atrocity destroyed the Albigensian heresy"—the heresy of private judgment—"and with that heresy the prosperity, the civilization, the literature, the national existence of what was once the most opulent and enlightened part of the great European family," says Lord Macaulay.

This same doom denounced against the Waldenses, the princes of the House of Savoy, as well as other princes, did their best to enforce. Serpents and wolves have never been more persistently hunted and slaughtered than were these Italian Protestants. Their patient suffering stirred even the serene calm of Professor James' philosophic soul. He recounts a long list of Waldensian martyrs who were burned alive, whose tongues were torn out, who were bound hand and foot and buried in banks of snow, whose mouths were filled with gunpowder and lighted by torches. He tells, too, of women impaled and carried long distances on sharp spikes.

When 3,000 Waldenses, in 1686, were ordered to give up their faith or leave the country, all fought till only 80 men were left. This remnant was sent over the

Alps into Switzerland. In 1689 came the so-called "joy-ous return." Eight hundred Waldensians, led by their pastor captains, fought their way, though at last re-duced to 400, to Bobi. The Duke of Savoy, breaking his alliance with "the abomination of desolation," as Professor James calls Louis XIV, restored this little band to comparative freedom, and their descendants live today in Torre Pelice and the consecrated Alpine Val-leys.

In the Church of Rome itself, longings for larger lib-erty have been felt. Mazzini, driven into exile, wrote: "The Church has been corrupted and must be reformed and led back to the simplicity and purity of apostolic times." He suggested calling an Italian council "To save the Church from superstition and infidelity." Pa-triots and philosophers, untainted with Protestantism, have uttered "a cry of pain" like Mazzini's.

A distinguished member of Parliament, Leone Cae-tani, in an open letter to the Pope, says: "We are not rebels; we are sincere Catholics, and, as such, we desire to stand up for the salvation of Christianity." He sees the Roman Catholic Church forgetful of the poor, servile toward the rich, mumbling formulæ remote from the moral needs of the present, holding only the illiterate masses and doing little to enlighten their darkness. "A religion to be true," he says, "must be the religion of all."

Not Protestantism, but Modernism, is the name by which this movement is called, so widely felt that Pius X exerted his strength to the utmost to crush it. But, unlike the infant Hercules, with heaps of strangled ser-pents around the cradle, Pius saw that he had failed, though the voice of these suppliants crying for reform

118

had a serpentine sound in his ears. The schismatics could not be strangled or silenced; they are living still. They may be found in churches and cathedrals, and even within the sacred precincts of St. Peter's itself.

In 1911, it is said, there were so many cardinals, more or less Modernist, that the Pope feared to call a conclave. These Modernists are fighting for life, but to them life without liberty is a mockery. They are devout believers in God, in the Bible, in Christ the Savior, and in the Holy Spirit. They cannot endure the sectarian and domineering spirit, the secularization of religion in the merchandise of sacred things, the elevation of authority to a point where it acts as a soporific to the soul.

As Italy received a national conscience, when freed from foreign aggression, so these Modernists hope she may receive a religious conscience, a Christian conscience, when she shall be freed from ecclesiastical aggressiveness. They dream of a day when there shall be a Pope called Peter II, a modern St. Francis, with all the sincerity and the simplicity of a St. Francis, but in closer touch with the intellectual as well as the religious and industrial life of these latter days.

This Peter, in the dream of the optimistic Modernist, writes to the King of Italy a letter throbbing with patriotism and deep spirituality. Leaving the Vatican, he takes up his residence in Castel-Gondolfo which, like the Vatican, belongs to the Pope. He orders the national flag to be raised on his towers; he purifies the Church, and brings all its teaching into harmony with the scriptures and Christ. Protestant nations, conquered at last, return to unite in the renovation of the Church and humanity.

119

A dream, we may call it, but a dream of "a new Heaven and a new Earth wherein dwelleth righteousness. "First, a dream, then a duty and then a deed; first, the far away vision, then a conviction to be obeyed, then the consequent and blessed reality," says a modern Joseph, a skilled interpreter of dreams.

In the stately funeral pageant observed in the Vatican last August for Piux X a great catafalque stood in the center of the Sistine Chapel. Four of the Pope's bodyguard of nobles in brilliant uniform were stationed like statues at the head and foot, relieved at regular intervals by four others. A row of cardinals in scarlet robes and caps sat on either side, some thirty in each row. Diplomats, senators, Roman nobles, Knights of Malta in striking costume, with the great white Maltese Cross on their left shoulders, and a few foreigners filled the space reserved for invited guests.

As the music of the choir of men and boys rang out among the painted arches the colossal figures on the ceiling seemed suddenly to become alive. Adam thrilled anew as the divine fire flashed from the finger of God. Eve straightened herself and stood erect, released from her warm prison close to Adam's heart. Prophets and Sibyls looked at each other with a wild surmise and peered down upon us as if, like the angels, "they desired to look into" the significance of this strange and splendid gathering.

May they not have seen in this entombment of a gracious old man, the peasant prince of the church, not merely the burial of a Pope, but of an epoch, the era of mediævalism, of autocracy, and clericalism, of authority for which there is no foundation in the scriptures of a human infallibility, an offense to man's reason and divine prerogative?

From their silent lips we heard in hearts of hope the prophecy that a new day is to dawn for Italy, better than the day of the Renaissance or the *risorgemento,* a new day for Roman Catholicism, better than the day of Hildebrand, a new day for Christianity better than the day of Luther and the Reformation; a day when "things which were cast down are to be raised up, when things that were growing old are to be made new, and when all things shall return to their perfection in him from whom they had their origin, even Jesus Christ, our Lord."

JAPAN AND THE WAR

"And the isles shall wait for his law."—Isaiah XLII:4.

When Commodore Perry's warships steamed into Yeddo Harbor fifty-two years ago the Japanese supposed they were at last looking at a veritable sea serpent whose massive jaws could doubtless swallow a city as easily as a shark swallows a shrimp. It would have been flatly inconceivable to the Mikado and his people that these ships were symbols of a civilization whose intellectual and moral splendor in less than half a century would swallow the deep darkness which had enveloped their land for three hundred years. For two centuries Japan had walled herself out from the world. All foreigners were forbidden on pain of death to pass that wall. No permits were issued to Japanese to travel in foreign lands; no ships were to be built large enough to sail in foreign seas; Japanese sailors wrecked on foreign coasts must stay where the sea cast them, or return home to certain death, the penalty of their misfortune.

It was the great privilege of the youngest of nations to awaken the venerable somnambulist from his long slumber. Like all sleepers suddenly aroused his eyes blinked with the strange and dazzling light. All his powers were undeveloped.

123

He saw with amazement that he must take his place at the foot of the class in modern civilization. His progress was so phenomenal that the Teacher forced upon him rather than chosen by him had to work overtime in order to get new material ready for the next day. In five decades this precocious scholar made up most of the lesson it took Europe eight centuries to learn. Japanese laws were revised and based on the Code Napoleon, probably the most lasting and valuable of all the souvenirs the great conqueror left of himself.   The school system including every village and hamlet was established.   Attendance on these schools was not only theoretically but practically compulsory.   Illiteracy is almost unknown in Japan—there are white men, it is said, living within walking distance of Washington who can neither read nor write.   Roads have been built across the land in every direction opening channels of commerce and communication in sections long completely isolated.   Railroads, with American locomotives, bind the great cities together.   Steamships ply not only through the Inland Sea, one of the most picturesque of the world's waterways, and along the coast, but to the entire Orient and Occident as well.

The army and navy are the pride of Japan.   During the last war they were the despair not only of Russia, but of France, Germany and England as well.   In none of her wars had Europe seen such prevision of all possible contingencies, such precision in executing plans, such reckless, dare-devil courage among mines on sea or land, such persistency in attacking fortifications seemingly impregnable as all the world saw in that war. In care for the wounded, and of all taken prisoners, a convincing evidence of high civilization, the Japanese War surpassed the best records ever made. The captured Russian soldier, if ill or hurt, became the nation's guest in hospitals where a nurse was provided for every two patients. All the rooms were decorated with cut flowers. The leading men of the district called to condole with the prisoners on the fortunes of war, and incidentally to take afternoon tea with them.

This is the Japan that Commodore Perry found asleep, a Japan now so wide awake that the long night of her sleep seems like a dream of ignorance or envy. Where once were only latent potentialities is now alert, tense, persistent, conscious and, it may be, relentless power. "The key of the eastern world"—and it may be of the western world as well—"hangs at the door of Japan."

This group of islands, a long, narrow strip with less square miles than some of our medium-sized States, is the Land of the Paradox to the Occidental. The Japanese alphabet is not a line of simple letters which any-one might naturally know, but a maze of symbols, each of which may mean much or little, according to infinitesimal changes which our eyes detect only by the use of a magnifying glass. These hieroglyphics are placed on the paper not with a pen, but with a brush, and the painter starts not in the proper way, on the left working to the right, but reversing the order.—Incidentally, it may be said this is the Hebrew method, far older than the Greek or Hebrew, which we have adopted.—Taught in this inverted way to read and write, a soldier naturally cuts with a broadsword, not by striking but by pulling, and a carpenter uses his saw altogether by pulling. A friend is beckoned forward with the gesture we use to an undesirable acquaintance who is to stay where he is, or to move himself away to a still further distance. The old men fly kites, and the boys look on approvingly or patronizingly.

Japanese houses are not their castles, solid and frowning, but are built of insubstantial boards scarcely thicker than cards. These buildings are lifted but a little way from the ground, and when thrown open to the sun and air look more like an elaborate pergola than a place of habitation. In these homes you sit not on a chair or lounge, but on the floor. You eat from a table six inches high innumerable courses, of which raw fish, with icing on it, will always be memorable.

Japan is the land not only of the Paradox but of the Picturesque. Everything is diminutive and delicate. The people are small. The common carriage, the Jinricksha, is in reality a perambulator for adults, hopelessly inadequate for the average American. Their horses resemble ponies. Their trees are more like etchings than the etchings of our best etchers. The hills are not offensively large—they do not frown on you like the mountains of other lands; even Fujiyama is threatening only when thunderstorms play around it. The snow on its head looks as if it would glady cool your brow heated by the climb to the summit far longer and harder than you anticipated, but under no circumstances would it chill your hands or freeze your feet.

Diminutiveness is wedded to delicacy—to material refinement which may be altogether physical or partly intellectual and spiritual. The faces of the jinricksha men, peasants and shopkeepers are round and not more

126

carefully molded than the faces of similar classes in other lands, but the faces of the more intelligent people, who are so fortunate as to inherit centuries of culture, are long and narrow, intellectual and even *spirituelle*. Simplicity is the keynote of their homes, habits and costumes. They reserve the ornate and grandiose for their temples and tombs, and they reserve the bizarre and ugly for their idols. They dress in soft grays and subdued browns.

With simplicity they combine courtesy—they greet the foreigner with a bright smile and a deep bow though they may not yet have learned "to greet the future with a cheer." They are ideally and charmingly stoical. Storm, fire or flood make as little impression upon them as upon the American Indian, but, unlike the American Indian, they are not stolid and remote. They are always "playing the game," and, whatever happens, they laugh. Those who have lived for years in remote towns have said when they came back to our work-a-day world: "We have returned from fairyland where no harshness or rudeness, no sour looks, no tearful eyes are to be found. We have been rolled backward by Time into Arcadia, and into the days of Pan-Hellenic festivities. We know that all our impressions are superficial and subject to revision, but as long as we are under the spell of this enchantment we can remember only the artistic perfectness of this Land of Paradox."

If Picturesqueness is the physical keynote of Japan, and Progressiveness the historical keynote, and Responsiveness the intellectual keynote, we must take Interrogation and Indecision as the moral and religious keynote. While Buddhism is the dominant religion, it has been rather an intellectual cult than a moral and religious force. Sir Edwin Arnold calls Buddhism "The Light of Asia," but at best it is a light scarcely better than twilight, in which moral distinctions are blurred and in which God, Man, Time and Eternity are so confused that the would-be worshipper has much difficulty in understanding whether he is not entitled also to be worshipped, or whether both worshipped and worshipper alike might not by mutual agreement consider Nirvana—the negation of conscious existence—as a state already entered upon, concerning which it was not worth while to make any assertions whatever.

The finest statue of Buddha in Japan, perhaps in the world, is the Daibutz of Kamakura. Christians as well as Buddhists, agnostics and atheists as well as mystics, have been fascinated by it, and after spending hours in contemplating the divine calm of that mystical face have found themselves drawn inevitably to return to question once more this silent sphinx. Before a god of such placid imperturbability moral qualities like truth, honesty, self-control and self-sacrifice appear "trifles light as air." The tragedy of temptation and sin; the struggle of the soul with demons that beckon it to the mad dance of death; the hope of deliverance from that which contaminates the heart and soul and not the hands; the perfecting of character begun in time and carried on in eternity are all matters of no moment or meaning to the Kamakura Daibutz or his devotees.

No people can rise higher than their god. So long as the Daibutz is the expression of the divine which satisfies the heart and soul of the Japanese, so long both morality and religion in Japan will be as pale and colorless as this stolid statue.

But the Japanese are capable of being stirred religiously. After Francis Xavier had made his venturesome way to Japan in 1549 and had gained an extraordinary number of converts—baptizing three Princes and twelve hundred of the people in a few weeks—the Shogun became suspicious that this foreign religion might be used for political aggression. The Shogun or Tycoon was at that time, and till 1867, the virtual ruler, though professing allegiance to the Mikado, who was kept in such seclusion that he was not allowed to appear even as a figurehead on state occasions. When the Shogun asked a Portuguese how his country had succeeded in making so many conquests so quickly all over the world, the reply was: "It's a very simply matter. Our priests first make converts and then we send our soldiers. The converts open the gates and act as guides, and the result is certain."

The Shogun was alarmed, as might have been expected, and began at once to plan the extermination of these intruders. They had already gained such a hold upon the people that little less than a war was needed to suppress the new religion, and two hundred years passed before its roots were entirely eradicated.

In the harbor of Nagasaki, called by many travellers the most beautiful in the world, there is a great rock, from whose summit a hundred or more Jesuit converts were flung into the sea, refusing to save their lives by the surrender of their faith. He must be bold or blind who can deny or fail to see the pure gold in a creed

129

that makes such heroes, though the precious metal may have been alloyed with base elements.

Signboards may still be seen in Japan threatening death upon all Christians. Such edits were on the statute books, like some of our laws, but fortunately not enforced, when our American, Dr. Hepburn, went to Japan in 1859. He was the first Protestant missionary to set his foot on her sacred shores. In his lifetime Dr. Hepburn saw Japan change almost as much religiously as mechanically and industrially.

Dr. Hepburn found from the first that the Japanese were not anti-religious or even non-religious. The religious talent had never been developed. They did not know what it was to be religious. The word meant nothing to them beyond the observance of certain festivals in the streets and certain ceremonies in the temples. That religion had anything to do with intensifying and ennobling a man's life in all its relationships was a thought that had never entered the Japanese mind—it was not to be found even in Xavier's teaching. There is no people on earth whose desire for perfection is greater than the Japanese. As they have gradually come to see that Christianity is the only cult or system holding this ideal as a possibility before man and commanding him to seek it, saying "Be ye also perfect even as your Father in Heaven is perfect," and promising him that he shall reach perfection if he will but take the path of repentance and faith—the appeal has come in the form most irresistible to the Japanese soul. Unconsciously the isles have waited for Christ's perfect law of love.

130

While tourists and merchants, and even students, of Japan assert that no European or American can ever understand the Japanese, both Europeans and Americans who have devoted their lives to Christianizing the Japanese say they understand them as fairly and love them as fondly as they do their home friends. "We never really know any one," it is said, "until we care for them," and while we think this a truism or a platitude applied to ourselves, it sounds like an impossible condition applied not only to all foreigners, but to everybody else not in our own set. How can we care for such uninteresting people?

That the Japanese are ready to meet us at least half way, with no weapon in their hands but a pen, was demonstrated in a novel manner a few years ago when the Commissioner of Education, who has the power of a Cabinet officer with us proposed to some of our educational representatives that the children in the Japanese public schools should write a friendly letter at least once a year to the same number of children in our public schools. Such a plan, could it be carried out, would change the so-called "Yellow Peril" into a golden harbinger of cordiality, confidence and peace.

If it be true "that the key of the Orient hangs on the door of Japan," it matters much that Japan should not "attempt the future with the past's blood-rusted key," but it is undeniably true that the use Japan will make of that key is in no small degree dependent on us. Japan still looks to her first teacher—America—to see how an up-to-date civilized nation ought to behave itself. The Japanese are an extremely imitative people and are most anxious not to imitate anything but the best.

131

They were almost as much impressed by our return of a large slice of the indemnity assigned to us for our losses in the Boxer uprising as were the Chinese themselves, and as they themselves had been in 1883, when by a similar act of justice the United States restored to Japan a sum our Government thought greater than was due us for injuries received at Japanese hands in 1863.

The Japanese know all about what we have done in Cuba and what we are trying to do in Porto Rico and in the Philippines. Our well-meant efforts at altruism amaze them, but they appreciate them, nevertheless, as a force even more effective than gunpowder. They will only attempt, timidly at first, to make any use of such a force, for they have many sad examples among our western nations of contempt for the intangible. How can we expect a people only half Christian, even theoretically, to be more Christian than Europeans who have professed Christianity for centuries?

Had Japan been in alliance with America she would not have been drawn into the maelstrom of this war. Had she followed American ideals she might possibly have had less territory ten years from now— though that is open to question—but undoubtedly she would have had more friends.

Japan's position is strategic for the military conquest of the Orient. She has had but little difficulty in loosening a favorite colony from the mailed fist of Germany. She may not have much more difficulty in helping herself to anything else she would like in China. But Japan may find, much to her surprise, that her position is even more strategic for her own conquest by Christianity. Whatever charges may be made concerning the Laodicean type of much American Christianity, no such charge will hold against the kind of Christianity in evidence in Japan's nearest neighbor and vassal, Korea. Neither can such a charge be made against the virile, aggressive and altogether modern Christianity advancing with giant strides among the students, scholars and officials of China. Nowhere in America would it be possible to reproduce such scenes as have been witnessed in China in the last two years. Specially constructed halls, seating many thousands, have been filled again and again the same evening by eager crowds of the literati, the class that considered Christianity till some five years ago a foreign adaptation of a one-time Oriental religion, possessing elements of interest only to the uneducated.

As the northern tribes conquered Rome, but were in turn conquered by Roman Christianity, so it may be Japan, the conqueror of Korea and the near conqueror of China, may find a Christianity coming from the East more convincing and congenial than a Christianity which they have thus far associated with the West. Japan, unlocking the Orient with that "key hanging at her door," may find a flood of light pouring in upon her such as Saul, the persecutor, saw, brighter to his soul than the light of the midday sun to his eyes—and, like Saul the one-time persecutor, Japan, once the sworn enemy of Christianity, may become the most persuasive and convincing messenger Christianity has yet found.

AMERICA AND THE WAR

———

"He hath not dealt so with any nation."—Psalm 147:20.

———

Many sciences played their part in shaping the land over which our flag flies. The geological formation of this continent is markedly different from that of Europe, Asia and Africa. Geologists lay much stress on the proofs they find here of one of their latest and most popular theories of the "crystallization of continents in triangles." A glance at the globe shows a vast pyramid standing on its head. A broad base at the North spreads toward its European neighbor on the East and its Asiatic neighbor on the West, while the compact head is buried in the mists of boundless Antarctic glaciers.

Isolated from the rest of the world by the ceaseless rise and fall of the life-giving waves of two earth-girdling seas, the resources of this continent are such that its isolation is really independence. Every product, mineral, vegetable, animal, which the highest civilization calls for is to be found here. Should the other continents destroy themselves completely, as they have already done partially in this insensate and savage war, this continent could supply a safe and comfortable home for all that might be left of the human race.

Geographically, as well as geologically, the part assigned our continent in the progress of humanity is clearly marked, especially to men who have been trained to read hieroglyphics of that sort. Here is what they call "the zone. of power," between the thirtieth and fiftieth degrees of latitude. Man may exist close to the poles. He may hunt and fish and eat raw meat and blubber, and drink whale oil in the arctics and antarctics. He may loll and sleep and "sweetly do nothing" but devour bananas by day and dance by night in the tropics. But to be a discoverer, an inventor, an author, a painter, a physician, or reformer one must live in the zone of power, north or south of the equator—preferably north.

A geographical error was the cause of the first recorded discovery of this continent. It is probable that Leif Erickson was blown out of his course and landed on our northern coast, but he did not know where he was, nor did he care. It was quite another matter with the Portuguese sailor who peered into the darkness on that August night in 1492 for some sign of a southwest passage to India. Could he find it he was sure of both gold and glory.

The Moslem had blocked the channels of Oriental trade through which wealth had poured into the coffers of Venice and Genoa. The tables would indeed be turned on the conqueror of Constantinople, who had laid sacrilegious hands on commerce as well as on Christianity, could an open door to Ormus and Ind be discovered whose existence had been suspected only by a few venturesome navigators. It was of this Columbus dreamed as he stood on the high forward deck of the little "Santa Maria" and saw at last the light flickering on the shore. Prophetic that light was. No American finds it difficult to believe that the New World is always to be a lightbearer to humanity.

Another science, ornithology, was given, seemingly, a minor role in our destiny, but still immensely significant, when a flock of birds flew by high in the air over the head of Columbus on their way south. Bancroft finds in these birds and the direction in which they flew the explanation of the original colonization of our continent. Columbus turned south, to follow the land birds, which doubtless were instinctively taking the shortest way to their feeding ground, and landed, not as his direct course would have led him, to Florida, but on Watling's Island in the West Indies, which he always thought was part of that India he had set our to find. But for this, Bancroft believes, our first settlers would have been Spanish Roman Catholics instead of English Protestants, and the history of North America might have been what the history of South America and Central America has been—and Mexico is.

We unconsciously and instinctively slur over all that happened on this continent till the climax of colonization when the Puritans landed in Plymouth on December 21, 1620. Celebrated in song, story and much conviviality, this landing has thrown into the shade the landing of Balboa on the Isthmus of Panama more than a hundred years before, of Cortez on the coast of Mexico and the conquest of Montezuma and his hundreds of thousands of Indians by a few hundred Spaniards, the founding of the Mission of St. Augustine in 1665; the coming of Sir Humphrey Gilbert and Sir Walter Raleigh in 1584; the excursion into Buzzard's Bay of Bartholomew Gosnold and his shipload gathering sassafras root and cedar logs—and enthusiasm with which he aroused James I to send two companies into Virginia. We forget the catastrophe at Jamestown in 1610, and the Representative Assembly with its first suggestions of a government "of, by and for the people," on July 30, 1619.

When we remember all this, Plymouth loses its priority but not its splendor or significance. The New England Colonies added an element needed for the crystallization first, of a confederation, and then of a constitutional republic. Without New England and the iron of its Puritanism, no element of sufficient strength could have been found in the Southern Colonies to bind the separate timbers into a solid structure. Puritanism may not now be in England the dominant force it was in the days of the English Reformation, when, as John Richard Greene says in his Short History, it made the English a people of one book, the Bible; or, as it was in New England, when it made the colonists, if not the people of one book, yet the people of one flag and one purpose. But for an American to sneer at Puritanism is not only to sneer at the hole of the pit from which we were digged, it is to sneer as well at the only hand that was strong enough to pull such a dead weight out of so deep a pit.

Now that Geography, Geology, and Ornithology, all providentially directed, have done so much for America, it should not be difficult for every American to express himself in David's words: "He hath not dealt so with any nation."

No other nation has such Possessions as ours. We speak of them not as a ground for boasting, but as a background against which our prosperity is made visible. The art of drawing maps is fortunately not among

138

the lost arts of a Golden Age lying far in the past. It is an art discovered since most of us were in school, and ought to be more interesting even than those ingenious puzzles which are so fascinating both to the old and the young. Any American child or man must feel his heart swell and his eyes grow big as on the map of the United States he places the map of China and finds that it does not cover all the territory lying west of the Mississippi, but leaves room enough for Japan in California. Norway and Sweden fit into Arizona and New Mexico. Great Britain, and European Turkey as it was before the Balkan War—it may not be as large as the District of Columbia when this war is over—Switzerland, Denmark, Portugal and Palestine may all go into Texas—that State which sends more daughters to Washington schools than any other. There is room enough for Austria in the Lake States of Wisconsin and Michigan and the Central Western States of Illinois and Indiana. France may be put into New England, New York, Pennsylvania and Ohio. Germany into the two Virginias, Kentucky, Tennessee and North Carolina. Spain into South Carolina, Georgia, Alabama, Mississippi and part of Louisiana. Italy into Florida. Belgium, Holland and Greece into Arkansas. Each of these empires, kingdoms, republics, would gain in resources by exchanging the territory it now has for territory of the same size here in our own land.

Our Pecuniary Possessions are still more impressive. Our wealth in 1850 was seven billions of dollars. In 1904 it was one hundred and seven billions of dollars. In 1905 Mr. Bryce said: "The Republic is as wealthy as any two of the greatest European nations." A conservative estimate of the wealth of our country in 1960 is six hundred and seven billions. Call that too large by half, if you like, and it will still equal the present wealth of Great Britain, France, Germany, Russia, Austria-Hungary, Italy, the Netherlands, Switzerland, and Spain, all combined.

The People to whom these possessions belong number about one hundred million. A hundred years hence they will outnumber, it is estimated, all the people of Continental Europe. These millions are not all philosophers or philanthropists, neither are they "mostly fools," as Carlyle, in a fit of indigestion, called the English. They make the strangest composite the world has seen. "The most disagreeable composite," some think it, when we are too neutral to serve their purpose. "The most promising composite," others say, when we don't happen to tread on their prejudices.

An Englishman who professes to have been present in the laboratory of the Universe during a discussion of the question of races, says he overheard Nature say: "Thus far the English is the best race I have made. Put in a few more drops of nervous energy and make the American." Whether or not the American inherits more vital energy than the European, he ought, at least, to inherit a better balance of power. There should be a minute and invisible gyroscope in every drop of his blood, keeping his head level whatever may be the elevations or depressions of the road over which he walks or runs. He has in his veins not only the Norman, Saxon and Danish blood, of which Tennyson boasted when he welcomed the Princess of Wales from her Northern home, but he has in addition a mixture of almost every other kind of blood that has ever flowed through a human heart.

As the commingling of metals forms a combination so slightly contracted by cold or expanded by heat that the compound is called an expansive balance, and a watch so furnished ticks on apparently indifferent as to whether it is hung in a refrigerator or an oven, so the pure-blooded American—though his great-grandfather may have been a German and his great-grandmother a Russian, neither of whom knew a word of English—inherits from his mixed ancestry the qualities both of the gyroscope and the expansive balance. He should stand straight where other men stumble, he should be both calm and cheerful in the enervating south wind of prosperity and the freezing winds of adversity and disaster fresh from the death-like glaciers of the north.

The Principles of this people in possession of this territory bear only a family resemblance to the principles of the original colonists, but all are alike in their love of Liberty and Equality. If either is lacking or remarkably deficient in size, we have difficulty in believing, however loud his protest, that the man is an American. The hyphenated name may have a German, Polish or Hungarian termination and he may be allowed to pass unchallenged so long as Liberty and Equality are hyphenated together and visibly incorporated in his principles.

Equality is the first-born child of liberty. Wherever all men have the free and inalienable right of "life, liberty and the pursuit of happiness," they are compelled to respect each other as alike proprietors of possessions so vast that all minor distinctions disappear. America has been called "The first successful attempt in recorded history to get a healthy, national equality which would reach down to the foundations of the state and to the great masses of men."

The American Purpose should be as clearly visible to American eyes and to the eyes of all the world as American principles or possessions. Only the Pilgrims and the Puritans among all the colonists, except the Quakers in Pennsylvania, had a distinctively religious purpose in turning their backs on the Old World and their faces toward the New. But Washington, and the men who fought with him to gain independence and to forge into a Nation the separate iron particles heated in a furnace of the Revolution, saw far beyond the moment in which they lived and the boundaries of the Republic they had formed. They realized that this was to be humanity's last great experiment in ridding itself of the incubus of mediævalism in State and Church.

Nothing could have been more offensive to them than an attempt to build a Chinese wall around their possessions, shutting out forever all who were so unfortunate as not to have entered before the gates of mercy and hope closed on mankind. They welcomed to a share of these possessions every people already sharing or desiring to share the American principle of liberty that begets equality, that begets fraternity. While America can never be a refuge for the anarchist or the nihilist, or for anyone who comes with the intention of wiping his feet on our laws and principles, it can never shut out, whether literate or illiterate, the normal healthy man, woman or child who thinks of this as the Land of

Promise. Humanity may be sure to find here a resting place for the sole of its foot, and air to breathe, and bread to eat, and books to read, and schools to teach how books are read. It may count here on fields and factories in which to work, and on laws so fair and just that all who want work shall have it and all who do work shall get enough out of their work to support themselves and their families in decency and comfort.

The Great War has stimulated our natural sensitiveness almost to the point of nervousness. We are anxious about our defences. Covetous eyes may soon be upon our possessions. Are we able on land and on sea to protect them? But our principles and purposes remain as they have always been. Should we attempt a war of conquest, and succeed, the results to Americanism would be scarcely less disastrous than a decisive defeat. We hold the proud position of almoner to humanity. We make good the claim when we act the part of benefactor. Lord Bryce said the other day: "No people exceeds, if indeed any people quite equals, the people of America in compassionate sensitiveness for suffering, and in the open-handed generosity with which they hasten to relieve it. Their love of liberty is equalled only by their sense of human brotherhood." We are very ambitious. We covet a throne higher than that of almoner—the throne of the peacemaker. We hope we do not lay a too flattering unction to our souls when we confess our belief that we possess qualifications inferior to none for this high position.

The chiefest of these is our perfect hatred of war and the spirit that produces it. We hate militarism and navalism, Cæsarism and Napoleonism, with the same

143

perfect hatred, whatever may be the language of the false tongues of their advocates. We see in every such "ism" a blow fatal alike to the family and the state, to civilization and Christianity. We see how complete already has been the sacrifice to this Moloch by some of the European nations.

First the family, as God intended it to be, was offered to this monster. An officer of the army—and every young man of good birth must be an officer—can only marry a woman with an adequate income. This military "Coelebs in search of a wife" is looking not for a godly woman, but for a goodly fortune. Whether the possessor of the fortune be Jew or Gentile, Roman Catholic or Protestant, is a matter of very minor importance.

With love goes faith. Religion, like marriage, becomes a mere consideration of convenience. The individual is sacrificed to the state. The conscience is a collective conscience, over which the Sovereign is lord. Moral distinctions are wiped out and the only morality is national safety, prosperity and supremacy. These doctrines of demons have inoculated with corruption and death whole sections of society in Europe. What the harvest is to be we see already when we look at the battlefields where men are being slaughtered like sheep for a system which has such sway over their souls that they die without a regret for their worse than wasted lives. Against such a system and against such teaching, though it come from the lecture halls of universities, or from the pulpits of churches, every American is sworn by his birthright and his privileges to wage a war as uncompromising as Hannibal waged against Rome.

144

Man, even in America, is still only in a process of becoming. "He partly is and wholly hopes to be." When he looks within he believes that it is his own soul that cries out for war as the one chance for either heroism or exalted happiness. He is half convinced that only military music stimulates him to climb the highest peaks. Richard Le Gallienne speaks for something in all our hearts when he cries:

"War
I abhor,
And yet how sweet
The sound along the marching street
Of drum and fife, and I forget
Broken old mothers, and the whole
Dark butchery without a soul.

Without a soul—save this bright drink
Of heady music, sweet as hell;
And even my peace-abiding feet
Go marching with the marching feet.
For yonder, yonder, goes the fife,
And what care I for human life?
The tears fill my astonished eyes,
And my full heart is like to break;
And yet 'tis all embannered lies—
A dream those drummers make.

> Oh, it is wickedness to clothe
> Yon hideous grinning thing that stalks
> Hidden in music, like a queen
> That in a garden of glory walks,
> Till good men love the thing they loathe!
> Art! thou hast many infamies,
> And my full heart is like to break:
> Oh, snap the fife and still the drum,
> And show the monster as she is!"

Not only men, but women as well, have a sneaking conviction that there is no hero like the man on horseback. In their eyes the glory of the conqueror dims all other glory. Men are afraid that women, if they vote, will cease to be feminine, and women are afraid that men, if they do not fight, will cease to be masculine. If it were possible to distill all the heroism of all the battlefields that have stained the world with blood, from the first struggles of the Cave Dwellers to the fierce onslaught of gigantic armies in France and Poland yesterday, as perfume is distilled from gardens of roses, would that distillation equal in quantity or quality the essential heroism of doctors, nurses and patients in the hospitals; of myriads of toilers who earn with the sweat of their brow the bread which someone else eats; of clerks and employees, politicians and statesmen, tempted with what looks to them like wealth to waver by a hair's breadth from the line of rectitude; of mothers in nurseries and kitchens, over cradles, stoves, and washtubs, plodding on and pegging away, ill-fed, ill-clothed and in bodily pain; of young women in shops and offices, lured with jewels and banquets, with elaborate costumes and luxurious apartments, with well-appointed carriages and automobiles—when one and all, or the bravest at least, straighten themselves in the majesty of their self-respect and righteousness, and trample the serpent's head of temptation into the dust? We need not look far to find greater—though less spectacular heroism—than the heroism of the battlefield, or a substitute for war that will stimulate the whole soul more completely and call out the last ounce of strength more effectively than carnage.

If America is to fulfill the promise of the past, and carry forward to its consummation the purpose of Washington and Lincoln, she must have patriots who understand her principles and are ready to make every sacrifice for them. But she must also have saints, not of the ascetic or ecclesiastical type, not saints who are concerned only with perpetual supplication for the salvation of their own souls, but soldier saints who do not forget to pray, and who know they are communing with God when they are fighting in His strength and with His sword against every form of iniquity that contaminates and corrupts the soul of man.

SOUTH AMERICA AND
THE WAR

"I will say to the North, give up, and to the South, keep not back." Isaiah XLIII : 6.

The Panama Canal makes two continents of one, but eventually it will unify two long separated and diverse peoples. It is the realization of the dream that gave Columbus no rest until he had crossed the "ocean of darkness" and reached the New World. After more than four hundred years all ships may sail directly through a southwestern passage from Europe to the Indies. The ends of the earth are bound together with the sweet influences of unimpeded intercourse as irresistible as they are invisible. The Canal was intended primarily to be a highway for commerce, and secondarily for our warships, rushing as protectors from our Eastern to our Western shores; but it will prove more than a Culebra Cut, through the rocky slopes of our prejudice and ignorance as massive as mountains, and our self-complacency as unstable as sand. Argosies without sail or steam will pass through this aperture as through an open sea, and anchor, heartily welcomed, in many long-closed ports of timid and suspicious peoples.

European misconceptions may excite in South America no deeper feeling than surprised amusement, but American misconceptions, though no more absurd, are more irritating to the feelings of our Southern brethren. They are not only Americans like ourselves—they are the real and original Americans.

Americus Vespucius knew nothing about North America. Brazil was the only spot in the New World touched by the sole of his foot. The first maps of our continent applied the name only to that particular section of the South, and now we are courteously, and at times contemptuously, indignant when anyone south of the Rio Grande claims to be an American. These Americans of the Southland are in the same boat with us. They are in one end and we in the other, but both ends of a boat usually sink or swim simultaneously.

Our ignorance of these near neighbors, if not relations, is made still more offensive by the close resemblance it bears to indifference. These two, ignorance and indifference, are as alike as two peas to most eyes. We may plead, not without a slight blush of shame, that our ignorance is the cause of our indifference and that we are not so intensely ignorant as to be unconscious of it or unwilling to exchange it for something better. Each year it is becoming less difficult to make the exchange, for South America needs only to be known to be appreciated, and knowledge of the facts is slowly seeping down into even the lowest strata of North American stupidity. We are compelled to confess that South America has some points of superiority.

Geographically, while we refuse to think even of European Russia as in our class, the figures compel us to acknowledge we are outclassed by South America. They have more arable land than we. Alexander Von Humboldt said as he sailed up the Amazon: "Here will be the center of the greatest population the world has even seen."

150

They have the loftiest mountains in the New World—the Andes and the Cordilleras. The widest plains—the plains of Argentina. The largest river—the Amazon. The greatest forests—the still unexplored woodlands of the Amazon. The richest mines—Potosi and Cerro de Pasco. The highest navigable lake in the world—Lake Titicaca. In less than one-half the time it takes to reach the Himalayas one may be on board a steamer plying across Lake Titicaca more than two miles above the sea, and looking with amazed admiration at Illimani and Sorata, rivalling the majestic splendor of the still loftier Himalayan peaks of Kunchinjunga and Everest.

Historically, the story of South America is much more sensational than that of the United States section of North America. The history of our colonies—from the Puritans of New England and the Quakers of Pennsylvania, to the Roman Catholics of Maryland—is soul-stirring and stimulating to the serious minded, but even modern readers, demanding a given number of thrills to the page, might find "The Conquest of Peru" up to their high literary standard. Neither Stevenson in "Treasure Island," nor Rider Haggard in "King Solomon's Mines" has imagined anything quite so extraordinary, incredible and impossible as the career of Pizarro. Fitting out at Panama two Caravels— the high-sounding Spanish name for the smallest sailing vessels supposedly seaworthy—this swineherd from Spain put 102 soldiers on board. They were all adventurers, as brave, bloodthirsty and greedy of gold as himself. With them there were sixty-two horses and two small cannon. After many hairbreadth escapes and sublime efforts, from the most sordid motives, they landed at Tumbez,

151

in Peru. So began a conquest even more amazing than that of Cortez in Mexico.

The country was exhausted by a fratricidal war in which Atahualpa, reigning in the north, had completely subjugated his brother, Huascar, reigning in the south. The Incas were bewildered by the glittering armor of Pizarro and his soldiers, and amazed by the war horses, so different from their diminutive llamas. They were stupefied by the lightning and thunder of the mysterious weapons of which they had never before even heard. They made a feeble and futile resistance, and Atahualpa was seized in the plaza of Cajamarca when he rejected the insolent demands of Friar Valverde that he and his people should immediately accept Christianity. His sacred person was loaded with chains, and he was held until his ransom should be paid—a room filled with gold to the height Pizarro could reach. When all conditions were finally met, a puerile charge was made against Atahualpa. He was convicted and put to death.

The history of South America becomes less interesting to the sensationalist after the completion of Pizarro's conquest, which, under the Spanish Conquistadores who followed him, brought the entire continent, from the Isthmus to the Straits of Magellan, under the Spanish flag—but it is more inspiring to the patriot. These republics have fought their war for independence like our own, but with far more reason, and with scarcely less heroism than that shown by Washington and his men. They were not able, as our colonies fortunately were, to combine all sections in a simultaneous revolt against Spanish tyrany, ten times more unendurable than the childish despotism of George III. Their revolutions went off like defective fireworks on the Fourth of July—spasmodically here and there, producing an effect more startling, if less splendid, than a single grand explosion.

Beginning in 1810, in Argentina and Chile, the series of revolutions was not completed until Bolivar's victory in 1824. Since Mexico closed the short, ill-advised excursion of Maximilian into the imperial purple and stained his regal robes with his blood in 1867, and Brazil ended the benign reign of Dom Pedro, the most democratic emperor that ever sat in an arm chair and called it a throne, in 1889, there has been no sovereignty from Cape Horn to the Canadian border, except the sovereignty of the people.

Linguistically, South America is far more interesting and diversified than the United States. We have, and care to have, only one language. We have no thought we cannot express better in our mother tongue than in the mother tongue of any other people. This is a serious commercial handicap. Selling goods is a slow process by the sign language. While South America starts with a linguistic capital only twice as large as ours, as far as the European element is concerned, Portuguese in Brazil, and Spanish everywhere else, no descendants of Europeans consider themselves educated unless they speak and write three languages besides their own. The native population preserve tongues like our Indian dialects, but more elaborate, running back to peoples in possession of the country before Manco Capac and his wife emerged from the waves of Lake Titicaca, like the Greek goddess Aphrodite from the sea, bringing both the Inca religion and language with them.

Archæologically, as well as linguistically, it is South America, and not North America, that draws expeditions like those of our own National Geographic Society to make long, tiresome and dangerous journeys into the depths of mountain ranges, where even prospectors for precious metals have never before pushed their way. Deep hidden, in our Twentieth Century world they found, in 1912, the half mythical city of Machu Picchu, built and inhabited by a race more ancient and more civilized than the Incas of Peru or the Aztecs of Mexico. "In the year 2000," says an archæologist, "when the Tyrol and the Abruzzi, Dalmatia and Carinthia have lost their Old World character, travellers may be seeking the towns hidden away in the Andes, Cajamarca, Huancavellica, Andahuayias and Ayacucho, for rare bits of mediæval life, untarnished by the breath of modernism."

Architecturally and æsthetically, South America can not claim any superiority. It is true Buenos Ayres boasts the finest Jockey Club in the world, built and supported by the profits of the race course, where betting is as legalized and systematized as buying and selling stock in Wall Street. Yet, in spite of the enormous wealth of this Club, the palace in which it is established is merely gorgeous—incomparably inferior, architecturally, to our Congressional Library. Everything else in South America, in Rio as well as in Buenos Ayres, wonderful as it is when all is considered belongs to the category that condemns itself with the faint praise of being "as good as" similar structures in Washington, New York, Paris or Vienna.

154

They are as ready in South America to confess our superiority in any particular when convinced of it, as we are to confess theirs. They acknowledge that we surpass them Mechanically. Yankees—as they call us all, using the term ordinarily in a complimentary sense —have built all their trolley, telephone, and electric light plants. Yankees have sunk their mines, taking out millions, and paying in taxes no small part of the expenses of the government in republics like Peru and Bolivia. Yankees have manufactured most of the tools and implements used in the mines and the fields. Agents selling the goods of Yankee firms make up a large percentage of the travellers who support the railroads and hotels. But for the supply stations of these firms, placed at strategic points in every republic, a broken mining or agricultural implement could be replaced only after the lapse of many weeks necessary for sending an order to the United States and receiving the goods by uncertain steamers.

Educationally, South America is far behind. Seventy-five to eighty per cent of the people in some of the republics are illiterate. Their educational system, an inheritance from the Spaniard, is badly balanced and tophcavy. The oldest university in America is not at Cambridge in Massachusetts, but at Lima in Peru, yet for a modern education the Peruvians go to Europe or to North America. At a gathering of thirty Peruvians, in Lima in 1911, all of whom were college graduates, there were twenty-seven institutions represented, mostly foreign.

The preparatory schools are very deficient in both quantity and quality. They are largely under the control of the Roman Catholic Church. When priests and nuns are the only teachers, the catechism and the Church Ritual will be the principal subjects taught. Familiarity with church services and systems count, of course, in such schools for more than acquaintance with secular history, philosophy, literature or science. Sarmiento—a name over which every lover of Argentina or humanity might well linger—was the first to see this fatal error, and to resolve that it should be remedied. Though not himself a Protestant, he sent to the United States for Protestant teachers from Wellesley, Vassar, Mt. Holyoke, and Michigan. They worked a revolution in the schools of Argentina. When opposed by the Papal Nuncio and Archbishop, Sarmiento, who was then President, sent word to the prelates that their passports would be ready at their convenience, but that the American teachers were to stay. There are many, though far from enough, distinctly religious schools in each of the republics, doing what the more intelligent Roman Catholics recognize as a most important work in raising the standard of education, and developing a class of men and women new to South America. These schools the South Americans desire to see multiplied.

Morally and religiously, the advantage has been on our side, not by merit, but by inheritance. The contrast between the civilization which the Puritans, Quakers and Roman Catholics, like Lord Baltimore, brought to North America, and the civilization, so-called, that Pizarro and Valverde brought to South America, is self-evident. Our colonists were seekers, if not all of them, after God, yet seekers all after liberty to worship according to the dictates of their own conscience, or not to worship at all, as they might see fit. South America was conquered but never colonized. The Conquistadores were not all as brutal and cruel as Pizarro, but there were few, if any, of them who did not share his unquenchable thirst for gold and his incongruous passion for making converts to the Church by the thumb-screw, the rack and the *auto da fe.*

Valverde was supposed to have had enough religion to qualify as Bishop of Cuzco, but he was absolutely ignorant of the religion of St. Francis of Assisi, or St. Catherine of Sienna, or of Las Casas, to whom all injustice and cruelty against humanity was a crime against God. Valverde had none even of Friar Olmedo's charity which made him restrain Cortez from the extreme measures he wished to put in force against Mexican idolatry. The religion of South America received the fatal image and superscription of Valverde. It was a religion that built magnificent cathedrals, costly churches, vast monasteries and nunneries, but crushed the conscience and the soul of men—a religion that could fire the soldier with fury against all his enemies, especially against heretics, but was powerless to stimulate even its priests to care for their people as every eastern shepherd cares for his flock.

Dr. Currier, a Roman Catholic priest, in a book published in 1911, with the imprimatur of Cardinal Gibbons, says: "Strange times those were indeed, according to our views, when bull-fights on the Plaza Mayor were attended not only by the vice-regal court, but by the religious community, and by the Archbishop himself. Bull-fights alternated with an occasional *auto da fe."* Dr. Currier lumps together the bull-fight and the *auto da fe*—the burning of a heretic—as rather trivial matters. The average priest today goes still further, and does not trouble himself with the amusements of his people, though his feelings are much more pronounced against heretics than bull-fights.

At La Paz, the capital of Bolivia, the loftiest and most picturesque capital, it has been called, in the world, a city hidden in the bottom of a canyon like the Canyon of the Colorado, whose walls are fifteen hundred feet high, there is every year an extraordinary festival in one of the churchyards. We saw a motley crowd of several hundred Indians, men, women and children, assembled after mass. They wore costumes usually kept for such occasions only. The skins of the llama and the vicuna covered their shoulders. The wings of the condor, with the head, beak and feet, were combined into a headdress. Their faces were covered with a Satanic mask. While the dancers beat a drum in time with a monotonous chant, whirling slowly around in meaningless circles, those outside the ring filled crude drinking vessels with a strong intoxicant, and urged the dancers to drink it down in a single gulp. All around on the brown turf sprawled men, and here and there were women as well —with babes in their arms—in the stupor of intoxication. The priests offered no protest. Either they are indifferent to the iniquity of it, or think themselves powerless to prevent it.

An intelligent priest in Santiago said to an American teacher: "We have lost the men. Our educated young men and professors in the colleges are all agnostics. If you can do them any good, we shall give you a Godspeed."

Nowhere in South America was there such a conscious throb of hope as at São Paulo. A snake, not unlike our blacksnake, called the Musurana, was held out for inspection either by sight or by touch while we were told about its nature and habits. The Musurana lives exclusively on poisonous serpents, and no venomous reptile can resist its lightning-like attack or escape swift deglutition. Where in all nature is there a creature so symbolic and prophetic of that day when all that is poisonous and venomous, all that is destructive and deadly in the universe, shall be swallowed up forever by forces as silent and sure as the Musurana of Brazil? He who has filled the heart of that wriggling serpent with unappeasible hate for every death-dealing reptile has assuredly sealed the doom, not only of the dragon, that old serpent that John saw cast into the bottomless pit, but of all serpent-like creatures, with the poison of asps under their tongues, who slime their way toward their innocent and helpless victims.

South America has suffered even more than we from this soul-destroying war. Hitherto Europe has been the great market for their nitrates, minerals and rubber, for their wheat, cattle and coffee. Temporarily commerce has ceased. Communication has been cut off. For the first time South America has concentrated her hopes on the north. We are eager to give her all the attention she requires. We will build a merchant marine to carry rich cargoes of our products southward. We will make any reasonable sacrifice for a reasonable profit. But there are many things South America needs more than the output of our factories which she will not ask us for, and for the lack of which she suffers uncon-

"All things grow sweet in Him,
In Him all things are reconciled,
   All fierce extremes
That beat along life's shore,
Like chidden waves grow mild
And creep to kiss His feet."

AFTER THE WAR

"Then cometh the end."—1st Corinthians, 15:24.

This monstrous war, which threatens to draw all neutral nations into its maelstrom, may be a sign that the end of the world is drawing nigh. It may be, on the other hand, merely an episode in the history of humanity, soon to take its proper place in the perspective of the picture which, when completed, is to tell the whole story of the career of our race on this planet.

Difficult as it is for us to escape from the impression of endlessness made upon us by this titanic struggle, it has, in fact, only occupied eight months, and this impression we know is a delusion. This dragon of destruction that draws its torturous length over the valleys and mountains of Europe, leaving behind scenes of unutterable desolation, must finally disappear into the bottomless pit. This conflagration, more terrible than anything the world ever saw before, must burn itself out at last when, like other conflagrations, it has consumed everything that can feed the flames. But before that—and it is for this we pray—the microbes of pride and lust for world power and supremacy which have inoculated monarchs with madness may be exterminated in some unforeseen way.

163

It is no longer possible to think in terms that satisfied our Greek progenitors, philosophers as they were. Homer and all the heroes of whose prodigies he has sung, were sure the siege of Troy began at a sign from the gods on Olympus and would only end when they had had enough of it. When the gods were no longer amused they would signal "Stop fighting." Had the modern Austrian Anchises, venerable and wise, and the German Ajax, virile and versatile, and the Russian Achilles, invulnerable except in one point not yet discovered, and the English Ulysses, a sailor by birth and training, and the French Hector, quick-witted and skilled in subtle devices whether of peace or war—had all these individually or concertedly looked for some sign from Heaven last summer before they fired the first shot, the sweet stillness of the world's peace would not have been broken.

The God in whom we believe, who is "afflicted with all our afflictions," and who watches with pity even the fall of the wounded sparrow, has looked on the beginning and the continuance of this war in which humanity is slowly being crucified with a sorrow like that which broke Christ's heart in the hour when Ignorance and Self-will crucified Him. When at last the end has come —may it soon come—and the thunders of this war rumble faintly in the far distance, many things now ignored will stand out clearly in the storm-cleared atmosphere on the sky-line of the world.

Humanity will be staggered by the frightful destructiveness of war. Pestilence and famine, marching together, can cause no such ruin as war. No plague since the dawn of civilization has claimed so many victims

164

from the classes most necessary for the progress of civilization as this war. "The Black Death" swept away a larger percentage of the population in the Middle Ages, but the first to perish were the very old and the very young and the weak of both sexes. War makes its first claim on men in the prime of life, men who have passed physical examinations as to their fitness. One such man, killed by a bullet and buried in a ditch, is a greater loss to the world than half a dozen unproductive men.

It is this type of man, young, strong, vigorous, fit to till the fields or to increase the productivity of the factory, that shot, shell and shrapnel are sweeping off the earth like insects. The Prussian Government reports one million, fifty thousand and twenty-nine killed, wounded and missing since the war began. This must mean, for the remainder of Germany and the Allies, close to three million—the combined population of Baltimore, Philadelphia, Harrisburg and Pittsburgh. And this war "will begin in May," says the commander of the English forces. The French have just equipped a hospital train with ambulances for the transportation of fifty thousand to be wounded probably in a single anticipated battle. For those who are to be killed no preparations are necessary. Devils in hell must rub their hands with delight. "Sherman was wrong," it has lately been said. "War is not Hell." Hell is a place to which Sin gravitates. All the fires of Hell are self-lighted. The innocent might walk in Hell as safely as in Heaven. But war is indiscriminate. No distinctions between guilt and innocence are recognized. It consumes warriors, women and children alike. There is no synonym in any language for war.

The destruction of property, as well as life, defies all figures. We talk glibly of hundreds of millions a day, of ten of billions as the total cost, but of what this wild carnival of destruction really means we have as little conception as a child has who watches the burning of a factory. The entire surplus of a century of toil is being exhausted. Treasures, too, for which there is no arithmetic or algebraic symbol, are being flung into the abyss. The amenities of life—those fine but hardly definable qualities that combine to create civilization and culture —are ground into the dust beneath the wheels of cannon and howitzer.

In the gashes called trenches, like gaping wounds in the breast of mother earth, are thousands of officers and men skilled in all modern arts, sciences, and inventions, musicians, painters, authors, mechanicians, but in their hearts there is room only for one hope—the hope of victory, which can only come, they believe, as men in similar gashes over yonder with whom perhaps they exchanged greetings and gifts on Christmas Day, are blown into the air or stabbed with bayonets. Between these trenches Barbarism holds sway as complete as in the jungles of Africa or in the forests of Europe before the days of the Roman Empire—and humane feelings are frozen into hate as little like philanthropy as ponds, filled with ice to the bottom, are like bubbling streams of clear water.

When this day of wrath passes, with it will pass the old order—it will not only have changed, but will have utterly disappeared. The map of Europe, as we have it now, may no longer be recognizable. Each of the warring nations is ready to make a personal adaptation of the old Persian cry:

166

"Ah, 'Power,' could you and I with 'Fate' conspire
To grasp this sorry scheme of things entire,
Would not we shatter it to bits—and then
Remold it nearer to the heart's desire?"

When that remolding is completed all our atlases,
geographies, encyclopædias and guide-books will be
scraps of paper unfit even for a rummage sale. For this
remolding Pan-germanism has one plan, and Pan-slavism a diametrically different one. Pan-anglicism has
still another, and Pan-italianism, which calls itself irredentism, advances the simplest and possibly the most
rational of all. Irredentism, as interpreted by Italians,
"ready," it is said, "to rush at any moment to the
assistance of the victor," means the redemption and
deliverance from foreign flags of all who speak the
Italian tongue. Carried out logically and applied to
all other tongues, it would cut deep into the present ter-
ritorial possessions of all the great European powers.
Could a wise, sweeping and impartial irredentism be
incorporated into international law, could kings, coun-
sellors and diplomatists consider language, religion,
race and "the greatest good of the greatest number"
as they "remold the scheme of things," there would
be scenes on this old earth as delightful to angels as
present-day scenes are pleasing to devils.

If this war is to end war, or to be the beginning of the
end; if, when peace is made, it is the intention and ex-
pectation of those who make it that it shall last at least
as long as the Treaty of Peace signed at Ghent a hundred years ago between England and the United States,
it will not be because it is "founded on honor," as Lord

Beaconsfield dramatically announced was the foundation of the peace concluded at the Berlin Conference of 1878. Every such peace—no one knew it better or cared less than Lord Beaconsfield—carries in its own bosom, puffed up with self-complacency, the seeds of future war. Things are settled, not when they are settled according to some code of honor, always superficial and never satisfying except to a little coterie, but only when they are settled right, not according to this or that man's way of thinking—Kaiser, Czar, King, President or Prime Minister—but according to the law of righteousness, as reliable, though not as immediately verifiable, as the law of gravitation.

No peace, whether concluded by professional or amateur peacemakers, will long endure in which the attempt is made to satisfy the souls of men with symbols instead of realities. This is the favorite trick sovereigns try only too successfully upon their subjects. They call stones bread, and when, by their royal command, the stamp of the official baker has been placed on pebbles, the people must take them at their face value with no signs of discontent and no complaints of indigestion.

This is also the favorite trick the world plays on its would-be masters. The unparalleled success of it of late years is the real cause of this war. Men in power, or who wished to be, were seduced by Satan transformed into an angel of light, into the belief that a difference in degree, though it may not be a difference in kind, often has the same effect. That while a single ordinary pebble, as any fool can see, is not the same as even a crust of bread, a handful of precious stones would be better food for a poor soul than a whole bakery.

168

Nobody is so idiotic as to believe that the life of a man or of a nation can consist in a few things. A diminutive shop, a doll's house, a shallow purse, a little territory, a few soldiers and limited power—but double these and then do it again, and keep on doing it—let the man get a colossal fortune, and the nation a brilliant place in the sun, and the whole outlook appears as different, as when the onlooker changes his place from a molehill on the plains to a peak ten thousand feet above the valley.

For forty years Europe, in a greater degree, and America, in a somewhat less degree, has tumbled to this trick. When this delusion had infected the Nietzsches and Treitschkes in the universities, and the Bernhardies in the barracks, and the contagion was carried down from the man with the crown to the man with the hoe, then all was ready and the merry sport began of catch-who-catch-can, and grab-who-grab-can—if only he can hold what he grabs.

Very industriously, scientifically, and effectively, the tares of materialistic Epicurianism have been sown among the wheat on which for a thousand years and more Europe was fed and nourished. The rank, luxuriant growth has choked the good seed. Humanity finds itself not only in a weed-grown field, but in a dense forest, through which only a little light from Heaven sifts its way. Men think it no longer worth while to look up. The horizon of their secularized hope is everywhere so near that it can be reached by a short run in a motor car. The sky is no longer remote, with great rifts here and there through which the eye looks into unfathomable depths suggesting Eternity. It is like a brass bowl over our heads, and we may easily know all there is to be known about it. The element of mystery and infinity has disappeared. "The mailed fist is on the spiritual aspirations of mankind and has made a treaty on his own terms with the human soul." "The world is face to face with a distinctness never before present with two great principles, the law of brute force and the survival of the fittest, made into a code of conduct, and the law of Christianity with its possibilities of a higher development and finer progress than brute force dreams of. The growth of the greater, through the sacrifice of the lesser, soul achievement at the expense of the flesh." To cry for peace when such conditions prevail is to cry for the impossible and the undesirable.

Thus far the world, though professedly Christian, has relied for peace on pagan gods. The nations have put their confidence first in Vulcan, the divine blacksmith, in whose smithy swords more marvellous than Excalibar are forged. In spite of church spires and crosses, Vulcan presides still over all the machine shops where the munitions of war are manufactured. Each nation thinks it a matter of life and death to be on terms with Vulcan; to get a monopoly of his latest inventions, or at least the refusal of them. Monarchs may sit in peace, "if not on bayonets," yet under the protecting shadow of the biggest guns that ever made earth—or a war lord— tremble. Through Vulcan relations may be established with Mars. The equipment furnished by Vulcan at tremendous cost should be to the god of war a pleasing acknowledgment of his supremacy. The people may sing praises and offer prayers to Christ, but wise nations put their trust in the strong old war god who always gives victory to the best equipped battalions

Great Jupiter himself, the father of all the gods, will nod his approval of Kings so practically and delightfully pagan. Pan, whose occupation was supposedly gone long ago and himself dead and decently buried, has come to life again—reoxygenized and stimulated with the pagan atmosphere of our times, and plays his pipe with all the fervor of old days when all altars smoked with sacrifices.

America relies on a different god. Neptune, the god of the sea, is our special protector. He will rise, we think, at our call of distress, and, with his tripod, transfix all submarines that may threaten our shipping. A blast from his mouth upon the enemy's dreadnaughts will make them turn turtle and disappear. While we still continue to sing "Our Father's God," let us rely on Neptune as our most trustworthy protector!

It is a far cry back to the primitive days when Moses asserted "a thousand shall fall at thy side and ten thousand at thy right hand, but it shall not come nigh thee," and to the days when David cried: "Righteousness exalteth a nation," and to the days when the prophet taught that the only city walls, altogether impenetrable, are the walls that are called "Salvation." To all these patriarchs and prophets, and still more to Christ, Jehovah was the Lord of Hosts, who holds in His hand all the reins of power. Great men of the earth may put their puny hands on those reins as we, when we were children, put our puny hands on the reins by which the horses were guided, supposing we were doing it all, though every turn was under our father's control.

The guidance of this world and the destiny of the race, has never yet been surrendered to kings or con-

querors. Humanity is being divinely steered according
to the chart of the Ten Commandments, however frantic
may be the efforts of ambitious men to get the wheel
into their own hands. They may succeed in changing
the course infinitesimally, and, intoxicated with their
success, may believe that at last human destiny has been
taken over by competent parties who have specially
trained themselves in anticipation of such a time. "In
nations," they say, "the sin against the Holy Ghost is
weakness." Weak nations, it is true, like the Greeks,
have ceased to exist but their addition to the world's
wealth has been imperishable. Not weakness, but wick-
edness, is the unpardonable sin of nations. Wicked nations,
whatever force they may possess, perish at last amid the
maledictions of mankind, leaving only a memory that
excites horror and dread.

Humanity has slowly moved away from barbarism,
not driven by a club or pricked by a sword; not under
the impulsion of brutality and animalism, but drawn by
sympathy, kindness, beneficence and love. On such
foundations the Home was built. Children lived because of parental care and self-sacrifice. Families combined into tribes, welded together not by force or hate,
but by mutual interest and fellow feeling. Tribes
became communities, dukedoms kingdoms, and republics, because in such unities only could safety and the
satisfaction of human instincts for social pleasures be
found. States have voluntarily federated themselves
into a nation, not without the surrender on the part
of each of both prejudice and liberty, but with the complete confidence that by such a surrender far more than
compensating gain could be secured.

A nation of states on this side of the sea has proved, by a hundred and thirty-nine years of unexampled prosperity that a union of states founded on the will of the people is more enduring and effective than any conceivable union of provinces founded on the will of an autocrat. "The United States of Europe" is not a meaningless term. Poets have sung about it and statesmen have discussed it, but the necessity for it has never been so evident as in the lurid glare of this war, and the possibility of it has never been so bright in all the history of humanity as it will be to myriads of praying souls—after the war.

THE END

www.ingramcontent.com/pod-product-compliance
Lightning Source LLC
Chambersburg PA
CBHW031300090426
42742CB00007B/541